NEW TESTAMENT GUIDES

General Editor
A.T. Lincoln

COLOSSIANS AND PHILEMON

D0141477

COLOSSIANS AND PHILEMON

John M.G. Barclay

Sheffield Academic Press

Copyright © 1997 Sheffield Academic Press

Published by Sheffield Academic Press Ltd
Mansion House
19 Kingfield Road
Sheffield S11 9AS
England

Printed on acid-free paper in Great Britain
by The Cromwell Press
Melksham, Wiltshire

British Library Cataloguing in Publication Data

A catalogue record for this book is available
from the British Library

ISBN 1-85075-818-2

Contents

Acknowledgments

This Guide is a thoroughly Glaswegian product, even if it is published in Sheffield. In preparation for writing it, I taught Colossians and Philemon to a class of Divinity students at Glasgow University, and I owe much to their suggestions, puzzled looks and penetrating questions. I am pleased to dedicate this book to that class of '94–'95, though it has appeared too late to help them in their exams! One of that class, Alistair May, has kindly read through the MS, while my Glasgow colleague, Alastair Hunter, let me see his unpublished paper, 'Mozart, Rembrandt, Moses and Saussure: The Lure of Pseudonymity', which helped to shape Chapter 2. Some readers may wonder whether the final chapter indicates that 'the Clydeside Reds have got me', but in fact it owes more to my ancestry, which includes numerous Quakers and one Thomas Fowell Buxton, a close associate of William Wilberforce, who is known to Barclays and Buxtons as 'The Liberator'. But perhaps the Glaswegian readiness to question authority, imbibed over twelve years of residence, has reinforced the subtle power of that hereditary spirit.

Abbreviations

ABD	D.N. Freedman (ed.), *Anchor Bible Dictionary*
ANRW	*Aufstieg und Niedergang der römischen Welt*
BibSem	The Biblical Seminar
CGTC	Cambridge Greek Testament Commentary
CNT	Commentaire du Nouveau Testament
EBib	Etudes bibliques
EKKNT	Evangelisch-Katholischer Kommentar zum Neuen Testament
HNT	Handbuch zum Neuen Testament
HTKNT	Herders theologischer Kommentar zum Neuen Testament
HTR	*Harvard Theological Review*
ICC	International Critical Commentary
JBL	*Journal of Biblical Literature*
JSNT	*Journal for the Study of the New Testament*
JTS	*Journal of Theological Studies*
KEK	Kritisch-exegetischer Kommentar über das Neue Testament
NCB	New Century Bible
NICNT	New International Commentary on the New Testament
NIGTC	The New International Greek Testament Commentary
NRSV	New Revised Standard Version
NTS	*New Testament Studies*
REB	Revised English Bible
TNTC	Tyndale New Testament Commentaries
ZNW	*Zeitschrift für die neutestamentliche Wissenschaft*

1

INVITATION TO COLOSSIANS
AND PHILEMON

There are two possible uses of guidebooks. When you visit an art exhibition or a historic building, you may buy a guide, but are then faced with a choice: will you study the guidebook first, before you look at the next painting or visit the next room, or will you look first and read the guide later? This guide is designed to be used in the latter way. It concerns two pieces of early Christian literature, and is intended not as a preliminary introduction to those texts but as an orientation to the issues that these texts have raised and continue to raise among those who study them. Thus the first and most important thing to say to users of this guide is, read the texts yourself, indeed, read them several times, if possible in Greek, if not, in a reliable translation (no knowledge of Greek will be presupposed here). When you read these letters you will be aware that you are crossing well-traversed terrain. They have been read, re-read, studied and preached for nearly two thousand years, and they continue to attract widespread and intense attention. Yet your own engagement with the texts is your single most important task, before you begin to consider how others have read and analysed them.

You may ask why this guide concerns the two letters, Colossians and Philemon. When you read them you will note that they are different kinds of letter, one to a church community dealing with communal issues, the other primarily to an individual, concerning his slave. But you will notice that this slave, Onesimus, the topic of the letter to Philemon, is also mentioned in Colossians (4.9); and further investigation will reveal that most of the names mentioned in the greetings at the end of the letter to Philemon (vv. 23-24) also occur at the end of Colossians (4.10-17). In both letters the author writes from prison, so that, on the face of it, the two letters appear to have been written from the same situation, belonging to one another as sibling products of the apostle Paul.

It is because of this literary connection that Colossians and Philemon have usually been studied together, and like this guide, many commentaries continue to treat the two letters together. Being so little, the letter to Philemon normally has to be included with *something* (though in some recent commentary series it has been honoured with a whole volume to itself); it is either lumped in with other small Pauline letters or attached, on these literary grounds, to Colossians. However, in recent years, as we shall see, most influential scholars have come to regard this literary connection as fictional; they take Colossians to be by someone other than Paul who borrowed the list of names from Philemon to enhance the credibility of his pseudonymous product. Thus Philemon is taken as Pauline, but Colossians as 'deutero-Pauline', and on this basis the combination of the two documents in this guide will look rather odd. Moreover, in terms of content, Colossians has much more in common with Ephesians than with Philemon.

My discussion of these two texts in the one volume reflects a traditional and pragmatic allocation of documents; it is not meant to presuppose anything about the authorship of Colossians, a topic that I will treat in Chapter 2. The discussions of the two texts will in fact be largely independent of one another, since, whatever one thinks about their historical origins, their foci are very different, with only slight overlap on the topic of slavery (Col. 3.22–4.1). They have also been significant to interpreters and scholars through the centuries in very different ways. It is worth outlining some of that significance at this point, as a way of introducing the varied topics that I will discuss in this book.

The Significance of Colossians

Colossians has proved to be an important document in the Christian tradition primarily because of its theological content. It appears that whoever wrote Ephesians (probably a 'disciple' of Paul) took his greatest inspiration from Colossians, for we find in Ephesians most of the same themes developed in a generalized mode; even the instructions on household life in Col. 3.18–4.1 have been taken over wholesale and expanded in the final chapters of Ephesians. In time, Ephesians, with its universal scope, proved to be more influential than Colossians, which has a more specific focus, and thus the prototype fell under the shadow of its copy (as also with the Gospels of Mark and Matthew). Nonetheless, Colossians was preserved by its inclusion in the New Testament canon. Although other New Testament letters were in some respects more weighty, Colossians was distinguished by its depiction of Christ, notably in 1.15-20. Thus it was in the realm of Christology that Colossians was to have its most singular influence.

In the patristic era, Colossians' descriptions of Christ as 'the image of God' and 'the beginning' who existed 'before all things' (1.15-17) were easily combined with the reference to the *Logos* in John 1 to enable theologians to present Christ in the terms of current philosophy. However, when Arius took the reference to the 'firstborn of all creation' (1.15) to indicate that Christ was himself a creature, the passage became the battle-ground of Christological controversy, with Athanasius and other enemies of Arius insisting that Christ was in a different category from creation, 'begotten not made'. Colossians thus proved to be influential in the developing orthodoxy of the 'two natures' of Christ, with special interest in its references to Christ as the image of God, and to the fulness of deity dwelling in him 'bodily' (2.9). The cosmic scope of Col. 1.15-20 also influenced Christian art, not least the image of Christ as Cosmocrator (world-ruler) which became a central feature of Christian iconography. The suggestion that Christ's work unifies or reconciles all things (1.20) was also conducive to large schemes of theology, in which the redemption of human nature was taken to be integral to the purpose of the Incarnation (Irenaeus) and the eventual restoration of the universe was suggested as its final goal (Origen).

The polemical edge to Colossians, in warning against 'philosophy' and 'empty deceit', has sometimes seemed to reduce the applicability of the letter, but it has also invited interpreters to 'actualize' its meaning by harnessing the letter for their own polemical ends. Thus John Chrysostom used Colossians to criticize contemporary 'angel cults' (see 2.18), and he and others made use of the depiction of Jewish practices as a 'shadow' (2.16-17) to represent Judaism as a preliminary and outmoded religion. The attack on ascetic practices in Colossians (2.20-23) was ready ammunition for those who objected to Christian asceticism, and in general the stress in the letter on the all-sufficiency of Christ has proved useful to any who felt that the Christian gospel was being supplemented in an unwarranted way, whether by the veneration of saints, the adoption of 'rites' or the practice of 'legalism'.

In the modern era Colossians has proved to be both historically intriguing and theologically controversial. Since the rise of historical-critical scholarship, the authorship of the letter has been much debated. A decision for Paul would require that Colossians be taken into account when assessing Paul's theology, but if the letter proves to be pseudonymous and post-Pauline, it would reveal something about the adaptation of Pauline theology in the generation after his death. Indeed, placing Colossians within the history of the development of early Christianity has proved to be an absorbing quest on a variety of fronts. There have been many attempts to identify the 'philosophy' against which the letter is targeted, since this would illustrate the cultural struggles of the Christian movement in defining its identity. Scholars have also investigated the traditions employed in the letter ('hymns', 'codes' or other early Christian material), which are of interest in their own right as relics of primitive Christianity but also for the ways they have been adapted by the author of Colossians. Those who consider Colossians pseudonymous have grouped it with Ephesians and the Pastoral Letters, analysing them theologically as examples of the development of 'early

Catholicism', or sociologically as demonstrating the increasing 'institutionalization' of the early church.

Theologically, Colossians has been a catalyst for some important controversies in twentieth-century theology. The cosmic scope of the claims about Christ in Col. 1.15-20 contributed to the attempt of P. Teilhard de Chardin to find a *rapprochement* between theology and evolutionary natural science. Subsequent interest in 'the cosmic Christ' came to a head in the vigorous debates of the World Council of Churches in the 1960s. In an address that took its starting-point from Colossians, J. Sittler challenged the Western theological disjunction between nature and grace, creation and redemption. In subsequent debates the Colossian image of Christ as sustaining and unifying all things (1.17-20) inspired innovative thinking about the relationship between Christianity and other world religions. Controversy continues to rage about the relationship between the cosmic dimensions of the letter and its historical orientation to the death of Christ and the community of the church. Some theologians have claimed that a theology focused on the church and salvation-history limits the ability of the Christian faith to make an impact on wider aspects of life (e.g. ecological concerns); others fear that a global affirmation of Christ's presence in the world is dangerous if the church does not proclaim the specificity of salvation through the death and resurrection of Christ. Colossians has also come in for some criticism from Paulinists who think it has blunted the cutting edge of Paul's theology, and from others who find its code of household duties impossibly 'patriarchal'.

Thus there is plenty in this letter to attract the interest of students of all kinds. Some will study Colossians with historical questions chiefly in mind, hoping to find in Colossians a window onto early Christianity at an important stage in its development. Others will have theological interests in a letter that continues to play its part within the Christian canon. I will attempt here to engage both kinds of interest, though historical questions will be handled first. An obvious starting-point is the question of authorship (Chapter 2), which will lead into that other historical conundrum, the target of the letter (Chapter 3). In both cases I will try to represent the alternatives as fairly as possible; rather than lead in one direction or another, I prefer to set out the relevant data and encourage readers to make their own judgments. As for the content of the letter, rather than exegete or paraphrase the whole (tasks amply performed by commentaries), I will focus on two of the most important passages, namely the 'hymn' in 1.15-20 and the 'household code' in 3.18–4.1 (Chapter 4). Finally, I will analyse the main theological themes of Colossians, indicating how they cohere and suggesting how they might relate to contemporary Christian concerns (Chapter 5).

The Significance of Philemon

In contrast to Colossians, Philemon has received little attention in the history of Christian theology. It has always seemed the most insignificant member of the Pauline corpus, not only because of its size (only 25 verses) but also because it has been regarded as a private letter concerning a specific and purely ephemeral occasion, the flight of Philemon's slave, Onesimus. Although some other letters in the Pauline corpus are also addressed to individuals (the letters to Timothy and Titus), they contain some hefty theological statements and are concerned with issues of wide significance in the life of the church, while Philemon's letter seems theologically light-weight and of purely private interest. Even the recognition that a wider circle is addressed in the opening greetings of the letter has not dispelled the impression that we are here reading a letter relevant only to its original context. It is not surprising that, at least from the fourth century onwards, many have questioned what it is doing in the New Testament.

In the course of Christian history the letter has occasionally been used as a moral example: here Paul stoops to take on the case of a worthless slave, or here he shows how the law must be upheld and even a converted slave returned to his owner. But it is only since the nineteenth-century struggles over slavery (notably in Britain and America) that this little letter has taken on real significance, since it relates to an institution that became a storm-centre of political controversy. Even though other texts in the New Testament contain more explicit statements about slaves, Philemon was brought out of relative obscurity to be used (by both sides in the debate) as an example of Paul's attitude to slaves and slave-owners. It thus came to be at the heart of the debate about the emancipatory potential of Christianity and has retained that special interest to this day. For those who consider Colossians and Ephesians deutero-Pauline, this letter to Philemon and the brief comments in 1 Cor. 7.20-24 remain the *only* witness to Paul's stance on slavery.

The very specificity of the letter naturally encourages attempts to reconstruct the story behind it, and although the consensus has long held to the theory that Onesimus ran away from his owner, alternative reconstructions have been offered in recent years. The rise of interest in the 'rhetorics' of Paul's letters, that is, their methods of persuasion, has also brought about renewed study of the letter, which has long been recognized to display some forceful forms of flattery and manipulation. Thus our first step in the analysis of Philemon will be to examine the story behind the letter and its argumentative strategy (Chapter 6). We will then address the question of Paul's reaction to slave conditions, looking first at the possible intended outcome of the letter, before stepping back to observe the variety of theological perspectives that have influenced interpreters of this letter (Chapter 7). At this point readers will find that it is hard to discuss such matters dispassionately, and they should not resist being drawn into engagement with the letter and the moral and theological issues it raises.

Further Reading

Surveys of the history of interpretation of Colossians may be found in the commentaries by Schweizer (English) and Gnilka (German), and of Philemon in that by Stuhlmacher (German); see the list of commentaries below. Sittler's address to the World Council of Churches was published in *The Ecumenical Review* 14 (1961–62), pp. 177-87.

Commentaries on Colossians and Philemon
The most useful commentaries available in English are:

Abbott, T.K., *A Critical and Exegetical Commentary on the Epistles to the Ephesians and to the Colossians* (ICC; Edinburgh: T. & T. Clark, 1897). On the Greek text; a wealth of detail but inevitably somewhat dated.

Bruce, F.F., *The Epistles to the Colossians, to Philemon, and to the Ephesians* (NICNT; Grand Rapids: Eerdmans, 1984). Revision of an earlier commentary with E.K. Simpson, 1958; clear and dependable; from a conservative stable.

Caird, G.B., *Paul's Letters from Prison* (New Clarendon Bible; Oxford: Oxford University Press, 1976). Brief, so often lacking argumentation for interesting and independent judgments.

Dunn, J.D.G., *The Epistles to the Colossians and to Philemon* (NIGTC; Carlisle: Paternoster Press; Grand Rapids: Eerdmans, 1996). On the Greek text; the most up-to-date full-scale commentary.

Houlden, J.L., *Paul's Letters from Prison* (SCM Pelican Commentaries; Harmondsworth: Penguin, 1970/1977). Brief, but full of succinct and suggestive comment.

Lightfoot, J.B., *The Epistles of St Paul: Colossians and Philemon* (London: Macmillan, 1875). On the Greek text; dependable for linguistic comment and full of old world charm; an authority still worth engaging with.

Lohse, E., *Colossians and Philemon* (trans. W.R. Poehlmann and R.J. Karris; Hermeneia; Philadelphia: Fortress Press, 1971). Translation of German commentary of 1968; very full with valuable notes; useful access to mainstream Lutheran interpretation.

Martin, R.P., *Colossians and Philemon* (NCB; London: Marshall, Morgan and Scott, 1973). A little patchy, though on some topics very full and stimulating; mildly conservative.

Moule, C.F.D., *The Epistles to the Colossians and to Philemon* (CGTC; Cambridge: Cambridge University Press, 1957). On the Greek text; some valuable observations but rather brief.

O'Brien, P.T., *Colossians, Philemon* (Waco: Word Books, 1982). On the Greek text; format makes this a little difficult to read; very full though largely derivative; conservative.

Pokorný, P., *Colossians: A Commentary* (trans. S.S. Schatzmann; Peabody, MA: Hendrickson, 1991). Translation of German commentary of 1987; a little convoluted in style and in arrangement of material; a useful resource.

Schweizer, E., *The Letter to the Colossians* (trans. A. Chester; London: SPCK, 1982). Translation of German commentary of 1976; based on immense and original scholarship, but its condensed presentation and an uneven translation sometimes renders this nearly incomprehensible; worth persevering with.

Vincent, M.R., *The Epistles to the Philippians and to Philemon* (ICC; Edinburgh: T. & T. Clark, 1897). On the Greek text; rather dated but useful for details of exegesis.

Wright, N.T., *The Epistles of Paul to the Colossians and to Philemon* (TNTC; Leicester: Inter-Varsity Press; Grand Rapids: Eerdmans, 1986). Stimulating, though sweeping judgments lack detailed support; theologically fits the conservative series.

Yates, R., *The Epistle to the Colossians* (Epworth Commentaries; London: Epworth Press, 1993). Useful as an introduction, but the serious student will want to progress to something meatier.

Readers of French and German should note the following first-class commentaries:

Aletti, J.-N., *Saint Paul Epître aux Colossiens* (EBib; Paris: Gabalda, 1993).

Collange, J.F., *L'Epître de Saint Paul à Philémon* (CNT; Geneva: Labor et Fides, 1987).

Dibelius, M., *An die Kolosser, Epheser, an Philemon* (rev. H. Greeven; HNT; Tübingen: Mohr, 1953).

Gnilka, J., *Der Kolosserbrief* (HTKNT; Freiburg: Herder, 1980).

—*Der Philemonbrief* (HTKNT; Freiburg: Herder, 1982).

Lohmeyer, E., *Die Briefe an die Philipper, an die Kolosser und an Philemon* (KEK; Göttingen: Vandenhoeck and Ruprecht, 1964).

Stuhlmacher, P., *Der Brief an Philemon* (EKKNT; Zurich: Benziger, 1975).

Suhl, A., *Der Philemonbrief* (Zürcher Bibelkommentar; Zurich: Theologische Verlag, 1981).

Suggestions for further reading will be given at the end of each chapter. Comprehensive bibliographies may be found at the end of the articles on Colossians and Philemon by W. Schenk in *Aufstieg und Niedergang der römischen Welt*, II.25.4 (up to 1985). The most recent literature is listed in the bibliographies included in Dunn's commentary.

2

WHO WROTE COLOSSIANS?

Does it Matter?

In the ancient world pseudonymity (writing under a false name) was not an uncommon phenomenon. When the reputations of great figures were established, it was natural for subsequent writers to compose works in their name (including drama, philosophy, historiography and letters) which imitated their styles and continued their traditions. Thus we find clearly pseudonymous texts created by Greeks and Romans, but also by Jews and early Christians. The production of such works did not necessarily involve the mercenary or deceptive characteristics we associate with 'forgery' (see Meade [for all such references see Further Reading at the end of the chapter]).

In the modern world we have become fixated by questions of authorship. Whether in the realm of art or literature, we put an immensely higher (cash) value on the 'original' than on the 'imitation', even if their artistic value is indistinguishable. We have tied to the 'author' the notion of 'authenticity' and 'authority', such that a painting 'in the school of Rembrandt' or a sonnet 'in the style of Shakespeare' is greatly devalued by comparison with 'the master's work'. Accordingly, we invest great effort in distinguishing the 'genuine' from the 'fake'.

One of the characteristics of post-modernism, on the other hand, is the loss of interest in questions of authorship and attribution. The meaning and value of a text resides in the

text itself and in the reader's interpretation, not in the putative author or his or her intentions. Those who thus celebrate
'the death of the author' ask what difference it would make if
we got the authorship attribution wrong. All that matters is
the text and our engagement with it, not its origins in a
particular mind or context.

From the point of view of theology, the post-modern turn to
the text might seem very attractive, even liberating. After
all, to take our case, Colossians has influenced the church,
and continues to influence it, by means of its own inherent
qualities, not by virtue of its authorship. To be sure, its original inclusion in the canon came about only because it was
attributed to Paul, but it is hard to see what difference it
would make to the theological importance of Colossians if
that attribution was proved incorrect. If what Colossians
says is true, it is true not only because Paul said it. Thus
post-modernists and theologians might be tempted to regard
the questions we raise in this chapter as a waste of time.

Unfortunately, historical questions cannot be quite so
easily banished. The meaning of ancient texts cannot be
entirely divorced from their contexts, inasmuch as those
contexts can be reconstructed. Even post-modernist profes-
sors show some concern for authorship, as may be seen from
their reactions to student plagiarism! Christian theology
cannot be wholly indifferent to the historical circumstances
of early Christianity, and is rightly interested, for instance,
in the transition from Pauline to deutero-Pauline
Christianity. In the case of Colossians, the decision about
authorship affects our understanding of Pauline theology. If
it reflects Paul's mind, it would expand and complicate the
picture of Pauline theology we draw from the other letters; if
it does not, it represents a post-Pauline development, akin to
that which we find in Ephesians and the Pastorals. As we
shall see, many reconstructions of Pauline theology, and of
the development of early Christianity, are bound up with this
question.

However, post-modernist questions do help us to reflect
critically on our presuppositions. In the decision about
whether or not Colossians belongs to Paul we are not simply
'reconstructing' history, but to some degree 'constructing' it—

that is, creating an image of Paul and what it was 'possible' for him to say. The early church constructed a certain 'Paul' by accepting the attribution to him of the Pastoral letters; most modern historical criticism has constructed a different 'Paul' by judging that he did not write them. Thus it is legitimate to ask what is at stake in different constructions of 'Paul': in other words, we will need to observe what (perhaps hidden) factors influence the judgments of scholars about the authorship of Colossians. In relation to authorship itself, we might also wish to soften somewhat the hard lines we typically draw around 'the author'. The boundaries between an author and a close associate, or disciple, or well-informed imitator are not in reality all that clear and after examining the evidence we will have to consider how wise or practical it is to insist on definitive demarcation.

Trends in the History of Scholarship

The letter to the Colossians purports to be from Paul and Timothy (1.1) and uses the 'I' form on several occasions in describing Paul's apostleship (notably in 1.23–2.5). It is also signed personally by 'Paul' (4.18) after a lengthy passage of personal greetings (4.7-17) which tallies extremely well with the personnel listed in the letter to Philemon. Thus, for most of Christian history Colossians has been accepted as authentic. However, with the rise of biblical criticism in the early nineteenth century, the possibility of pseudonymity was recognized in relation to biblical documents just as in the case of other ancient literature.

F.C. Baur was not the first to question the authenticity of Colossians (that 'honour' belongs to E.T. Mayerhoff in 1838), but the student with access to a well-stocked library may still read his powerful arguments against both Colossians and Ephesians, which in his view must stand or fall together. Baur maintained that these letters represent a form of Gnosticizing metaphysical speculation that goes well beyond Paul and belongs rather in the post-apostolic era. The exaggerated claims for Paul's apostleship (e.g. in 1.23-24) and the peculiarities of the Greek style of these letters (full of repetitions and tautologies, 'so far inferior to Romans') further

confirmed his sense that the theology of the letters reflected
a later stage when the church was anxious to stress its unity
and universal significance (Baur, II, pp. 1-44). Baur's role as
founder of the 'Tübingen school' ensured that his judgments
were vigorously debated throughout the rest of the nineteenth century: they divided German scholarship, though
they were generally rejected by the more conservative
English-speaking scholars (e.g. the commentaries of
Lightfoot and Abbott).

A shift in scholarly perceptions arose from the work of the
'History of Religions School' (1880s onwards). Here
pioneering work by scholars such as R. Reitzenstein and M.
Dibelius showed that the 'speculations' in Colossians on
cosmic powers and the assertion of the universal authority of
Christ did not need to be relegated to a post-apostolic period
of Gnosticism, but could easily reflect the religious conditions
of Paul's lifetime. In the 1930s and 1940s Dibelius and E.
Lohmeyer wrote commentaries on Colossians in the most
influential German commentary series, both taking the letter
to be by Paul; and a massive monograph on Colossians and
Ephesians by E. Percy in 1946 further reinforced the
respectability of their position. English-speaking scholars
were content to find their conservatism thus vindicated.

However, by the 1940s and early 1950s the tide was beginning to turn decisively in Germany under the influence of
the Bultmann school. R. Bultmann and his pupils (e.g.
E. Käsemann, G. Bornkamm, W. Marxsen and E. Schweizer)
revived interest in Pauline theology, and the specific framework in which they interpreted it (influenced by Lutheran
and existentialist theology) was hostile towards aspects of
Colossians and Ephesians. Thus Bultmann found in
Colossians a less radical view of faith and eschatology than
he championed in Paul, together with 'a certain doctrinairi-
anism and moralization' in its understanding of salvation
(Bultmann, p. 180). Käsemann considered Colossians to
reflect a Christianized form of Gnostic mythology, which he
regarded as alien to Paul, and found traces of an appeal to
apostolic authentication which he took to be 'the voice of the
sub-apostolic age' (p. 167). Bornkamm had originally thought
Colossians to be genuinely Pauline, but his change of mind at

the end of the 1940s represents this shift in German Protestant scholarship. The theological investment in keeping Paul 'clean' from the 'mythological' or 'moralizing' elements in Colossians and Ephesians is evident in Käsemann's blast against H. Schlier, a Bultmann pupil who became a Catholic and started to defend the authenticity of these two letters: in Käsemann's opinion, Schlier's work meant that 'decisive elements in the original message and theology of Paul are curtailed and devalued' (cited in Lohse, p. 181 n. 9). Similarly, Schenk judges that those who consider Colossians to be by Paul only show what an imprecise hold they have on Paul's theology: to add this to the list of Paul's letters would be a quantitative gain but qualitative loss (p. 3349)!

Since the 1950s, despite the rearguard action of W.G. Kümmel, the vast majority of German scholarship has declared against the Pauline authorship of Colossians: Lohse's influential commentary (first published in 1968) is an obvious case in point. English-speaking scholarship held out rather longer, as one may see from the commentaries by Moule, Bruce, Houlden, Martin and Caird (spanning the 1950s to the 1970s). German scepticism was bolstered by a full-length analysis of the style of Colossians by W. Bujard, published in 1973. Since stylistic analysis can claim to be less subjective than theological evaluation, the case against Pauline authorship has often since that date been taken to be proven. Nowadays throughout mainstream scholarship (even English-speaking), Colossians is routinely bracketed out as 'deutero-Pauline': the consensus accepts only seven letters as 'assuredly' Pauline (Romans, Galatians, 1 and 2 Corinthians, Philippians, Philemon and 1 Thessalonians). Colossians and Ephesians are taken to exemplify a stage of development towards moral regulation (household codes) and 'stabilizing institutionalization' (MacDonald), a stance perhaps influenced by a desire to distance Paul from the politically incorrect sentiments of the Colossian household code (3.18–4.1). However, many Pauline scholars will admit that the case against Colossians is not nearly as strong as that against Ephesians and the Pastorals. Unfortunately, the work of those who defend Pauline authorship (e.g. Cannon and the commentaries by Wright and O'Brien) has a distinctly conservative air about it (and no doubt conservative theological commitments play some part on this side of the debate). In fact, the evidence for pseudonymity is not decisive, and strong arguments can still be mounted for Pauline authorship even if one takes a 'radical' view on other historical questions. If New Testament scholarship is worth anything it must proceed by evidence, not by majority voting. This overview of scholarship suggests that the grounds and moods of the debate have shifted somewhat over the decades, not unrelated to theological commitments. We may now examine in more detail the three main criteria for judgment: historical plausibility, congruity in ideas, and style. These are in essence the same criteria that historians use in relation to any disputed document (e.g. the famous 'Hitler diaries'). In the case of the Pastorals, they each produce results that argue decisively against Pauline authorship, but we must see how they turn out in relation to Colossians.

Historical Plausibility

Here the question concerns whether the type of document we have in Colossians, and the types of issues it discusses, fit plausibly in the life-time of Paul, or must be consigned to a later period. We may leave aside here one special factor that has bedeviled our topic since the days of Mayerhoff: the nature of the relationship between Colossians and Ephesians. Over the years several scholars have argued that Colossians was written in imitation of Ephesians or was interpolated with material drawn from that letter: either possibility would obviously rule out Pauline authorship of the present Colossians. However, the current consensus is surely right to hold that, if there is a literary relationship between the two letters, Colossians was used by Ephesians, not the other way around; that makes it possible still to hold that Colossians is by Paul.

Considering first the general character of Colossians, it must be said that in its shape, in its targeting of some specific problem (see the next chapter), and in its use of personal greetings, it matches what we know of Pauline letter-writing very well. In particular, a comparison of the greetings in 4.7-17 with the names listed in Philemon 23-24 reveals both a close matching and a wide variation in order and style. That suggests *either* that Colossians was written by Paul at the same time and in the same circumstances as Philemon *or* that it was written by a Pauline imitator who knew Philemon and was capable of very skilful adaptation of its names to make Colossians look authentic. There are small differences between the two lists, but these are more easily explained by real circumstances than by a subtle fictitious use of the names in Philemon. To be sure, the Pastorals (which may be shown on other grounds to be pseudonymous) contain extensive personal references, but no attempt is made there to match these to an original Pauline letter. If Colossians is by a later Paulinist, it is unparalleled in its sophisticated adaptation of incidental details to camouflage its inauthenticity (contrast the wooden use of Col. 4.7-8 in Eph. 6.21-22). That does not rule the possibility out of court, but it gives one reason to pause.

As was noted above, it has been argued that the theology of Colossians, and the 'error' it was directed against, are only imaginable in a post-apostolic period of early Christianity. Such arguments should be treated with caution since they suggest a far more precise knowledge of developments in early Christianity and in its contemporary thought-world than is truly available to us. To be sure, the battle-front in Colossians is different from that discernible in other Pauline letters, but we are much too ignorant of early Christian history to be able to rule this *impossible* in Paul's lifetime. Unlike in the Pastorals, there are no signs here of developed church offices, and while Ephesians arguably looks back wistfully to an apostolic era (Eph. 2.20), nothing in Colossians is demonstrably anachronistic. (Kiley's argument [pp. 46-51] that the lack of reference to financial transactions is suspicious can hardly be taken seriously, and Sanders did not quite prove his case that Colossians shows signs of an imitator copying phrases from authentic letters.) Thus it cannot be said that there is anything in this letter that argues against its composition in Paul's lifetime: indeed Schweizer and Dunn, who both take the stylistic arguments to rule out Pauline authorship, nonetheless hold that Colossians was written in Paul's lifetime, but by an associate.

Congruity in Ideas

Until the use of the computer put stylistic arguments onto more solid statistical ground, the weight of the argument concerning Colossians rested on its theological compatibility or incompatibility with Paul (see e.g. Lohse, pp. 177-83). On this issue, those who argue against Pauline authorship usually assert that the author of Colossians has picked up peripheral Pauline themes and made them dominant in a fashion uncharacteristic of Paul, or that a shift has occurred that has taken Pauline thought in a direction he could never have followed. All the main themes of Colossians have come under scrutiny in this way. We may put them under five headings:

1. *Christology.* At stake here is not so much the centrality of Christology, but the exalted terms in which Christ is depicted in Colossians. We will examine one key passage (1.15-20) in some detail below (Chapter 4), but here we may note in general how Christ is accorded a cosmic role in the creation and reconciliation of the universe (1.15-20), how his universal sovereignty over the powers is emphasized (1.16; 2.10, 15) and how it is claimed of Christ that 'in him the whole fullness of deity dwells bodily' (2.9). Thus, in a striking way, the central mystery celebrated in Colossians is Christ himself (2.2) and there is greater reflection on the nature of Christ and his role in the universe than in any of the assured letters of Paul. It is agreed on all sides that there are partial parallels to Colossian Christology in the 'hymn' cited by Paul in Phil. 2.6-11 (on Christ's sovereignty) and in the 'creed' cited in 1 Cor. 8.6 (on the role of Christ in creation); there are also comments on Christ's role in relation to the powers in such passages as Rom. 8.38 and 1 Cor. 15.20-28. If Col. 1.15-20 is, as many think, based on a pre-formed 'hymn', one might imagine how Paul could incorporate ideas that he does not express elsewhere, but to many scholars the fixation of our author on such 'mythological cosmology' (Bultmann) is uncharacteristic of Paul, and the celebration of Christ as

already exalted over the powers is too far out of step with the cautious assertion of his future rule in 1 Cor. 15.20-28. That leads us to our second category.

2. *Eschatology.* The emphasis in Colossians is on *realized* eschatology. The Colossian Christians are assured that they have been rescued from the power of darkness and transferred into the kingdom of God's Son (1.13), and later they are described as having been both buried and raised with Christ in baptism (2.12), a motif that governs 3.1-4. As is well known, Paul expresses himself far more cautiously in 1 Corinthians, emphasizing the 'not yet' at least as often as the 'already' (e.g. 1 Cor. 4.8-10; 13.8-13), and in his reflection on baptism in Romans 6 he seems to go out of his way to *avoid* saying that the baptized have been raised with Christ: they have 'newness of life' (6.4) and *will be* united with him in a resurrection like his (6.6), but are not described as already raised. The question is how large a shift this represents and whether it occurs at a point where Paul would have refused to change his ground, whatever the situational circumstances. Some scholars have claimed that Colossians displays a tell-tale loss of interest in the imminent parousia of Christ and associated notions of judgment and resurrection. There are still forward-looking references (e.g. 3.4, 6, 24), but the Christian life is no longer lived under the shadow of the future as radically as in Paul. The dominant metaphors have become spatial (below and above, e.g. 3.1-4) rather than temporal (now and then). It is hard to deny that there is a different complexion to the eschatology of Colossians; the question is *how different* it is and whether it is unthinkable that it derives from the mind of Paul. The presence of spatial metaphors in the acknowledged letters (e.g. Gal. 4.26; Phil. 3.20) and the variations (or developments) in Paul's eschatological views do not make this a wholly straightforward matter.

3. *Ecclesiology.* The two themes thus far considered bear directly on this third, inasmuch as 'the church' is described in Colossians in relation to Christ and time in a way unparalleled in the seven assured letters. The metaphor of the church as the body of Christ (Col. 1.18; 2.19) is similar to that famously employed in 1 Corinthians 12 and Romans 12,

but in Colossians Christ is singled out as 'the Head', whereas
in 1 Corinthians and Romans the metaphor is not pressed in
that direction. Arguably what is at stake here is not merely a
shift in metaphor (hardly impossible for Paul, whose
metaphors are notoriously unstable) but a new conception of
the church as participating in the cosmic authority of Christ.
Has the term 'church' here developed a new sense, beyond
that of a local gathering in a house (a usage still found in
Col. 4.15), as a single universal entity that channels or
embodies the Lordship of Christ? The ecclesiology of
Ephesians certainly indicates a shift in that direction, but
some see the same process of development already operative
in Colossians. Once again, the question is whether this
stretches Pauline reflection on the church (e.g. 1 Cor. 3.21-
23; 6.2-3) further than is historically and psychologically
plausible.

4. *Apostolic Importance.* As is well known, Paul describes
himself in fairly grandiose (some would say 'self-important')
terms in his letters, as the apostle to the Gentiles.
Nonetheless, some statements in Colossians have seemed to
go further than is imaginable from Paul and to hint at the
(later) notion of apostolic church-foundation or succession.
Could Paul have described himself as 'the servant of the
church' (singular, 1.24-25) who 'completes what is lacking in
Christ's afflictions' for its sake (1.24)? Granted the use of not-
dissimilar language in 2 Corinthians (e.g. 4.7-15), could he
have generalized its application from his own churches to
'the church' in general? Further, could he have considered
the gospel to have been 'proclaimed to every creature under
heaven' (1.23; contrast the sense of an unfinished task in
Rom. 15)? Are these signs of a later age inflating Paul's apostolic role? And does the careful recommendation of Epaphras
(1.7-8) function, like some of the personal references in the
Pastorals, to legitimate the next generation of leadership in
the Pauline churches (see Marxsen, pp. 177-85)? Or are these
all explicable features of Paul's own style in writing to a
church he has not founded but for which he feels himself
responsible?

5. *Ethical Codification.* This last factor has only become
prominent in recent years. None of the general ethical

instruction in Colossians 3 is exceptional. Indeed, its presentation in the form of indicative and imperative ('you have died...put to death, therefore...', 3.1-5) matches exactly Paul's own style (e.g. Rom. 6.1-12). However, in 3.18–4.1 we find the outlines of a 'household code' (see below, Chapter 4), whose ethos is one of hierarchy and subjection. Is what is said here about husbands and wives (3.18-19) incompatible with Paul's discussion of marriage in 1 Corinthians 7? And is the instruction to slaves and masters out of step with the letter to Philemon? Is it likely that Paul would adapt a code like this, or is this a sign of creeping 'institutionalization' in the 'sub-apostolic' era? Clearly, our general image of Paul will determine our judgment as to the size and significance of the distance between Colossians and the assured letters.

It is inevitable that this combination of differences and similarities will be variously assessed by different scholars. Cumulatively it looks more significant than on each individual account, but still the question remains whether the distance from authentic Pauline theology is significant enough to require positing a different author. We have already drawn attention to the fact that ideological considerations may sometimes influence such a decision, especially the concern to keep Paul theologically and ethically 'untainted'. But there is also a methodological question about what range and variety we might expect from a figure like Paul. Scholars are now perhaps less prone than in previous generations to regard Paul's thought as consistent, systematized and neatly edged, but there is still the tendency to regard the seven assured letters as representing the limits of what is imaginable. Many years ago, H. Chadwick pointed out what 'an uncommonly ingenious controversialist' Paul was and suggested that 'the case against the authenticity of Colossians depends...above all on a capacity gravely to underestimate Paul's versatility and intelligence' (p. 271). Yet, clearly, some limits must be imagined and are applied quite plausibly by those who regard the Pastorals as the product of a mind other than Paul's. Even when allowing for the influence of the Colossian situation on Paul's mind, and the necessities of his confrontation with the 'philosophy'

there, it is plausible to argue that some aspects of the
theology of Colossians have moved too far from Paul to be
credited to him. But it is harder to prove such a claim. The
problem is that both sides in this debate are able to argue
'Heads I win, Tails you lose.' On the one side, the similarities
with Paul are taken to argue for authenticity, and the differences indicate only his flexibility of mind, differences which a
careful imitator would hardly introduce. On the other, the
similarities with Paul show the extent to which the imitator
was steeped in Pauline thought, but the differences indicate
the operation of a different mind. It is hard to see how such
an argument can be resolved.

Style

Arguments from style have played some part in the debate
on the authorship of Colossians from the very beginning, but
it is only in the last few decades that the question could be
rigorously assessed by the application of statistical analysis
(stylometry) and by harnessing computers for multiple and
large-scale stylistic tests. In the early stages of the debate,
scholars set great store on factors that now seem wholly
unpersuasive. Thus it was noted that there were 34 words
unique to Colossians in the New Testament (such are called,
in technical parlance, *hapax legomena*) and 28 that are found
in Colossians in common with other New Testament books,
but not in common with the seven assured letters of Paul
(see the lists in Lohse, pp. 85-86). But such statistics might
be simply explained by reference to the unique situation
addressed in Colossians, and an analysis of Philippians
would show still higher figures (without proving anything
about its authorship). Similarly weak was the argument that
Colossians lacked a range of words that were typical of
Pauline theology (see again Lohse, pp. 86-87). This would
only be a serious argument if Colossians was directed against
something very like the target of one of Paul's other letters
(this is indeed a major flaw in N.T. Wright's argument that
Paul here addresses something much like the situation in
Galatia). But if the topic of conversation differs, we cannot
insist that Paul always use the same language! In fact,

vocabulary usage (or non-usage) is an inadequate criterion
for an issue like this.

Fortunately, there are plenty of other stylistic tests which
promise greater objectivity by the fact that they measure the
whole character of the document including those elements
that represent a writer's unconscious habits. In Greek there
are a lot of little words—conjunctions and particles meaning
things like 'so', 'and', 'but', 'neither'—which are integral to
the language but not the sort of thing that an author (or an
imitator) would think much about. Charting their frequency
in a largish body of prose might reveal a significant discrep-
ancy. This was an exercise first conducted in a thorough
manner by W. Bujard in 1973. He also attempted to give a
more scientific basis to the analysis of the syntax of the letter
(how its phrases and sentences are put together). It had often
been observed that some of the sentences in Colossians were
extremely long and that their style was rather loose, with
repetitions, near synonyms and the piling up of expressions.
For instance, Col. 1.3-8 is all one long sentence in the original Greek, with apparent synonyms like 'bearing fruit and
growing' (1.6) and the piling up of phrases like 'the word of
truth, the gospel' (1.5). Bujard also examined the 'rhetorical
engagement' of the letter, that is, how it argues and
advances its thought. Students can gain access to some of
Bujard's work in the discussion by Kiley (pp. 51-59), where it
will be seen that Bujard tried to give his results a numerical
value and to compare percentages with the seven assured
letters. In some cases, he found Colossians to fall within the
range of usage found in those letters (it is often closest to
Philippians), but in a number of others it stands out on its
own. Bujard took his research to prove, on a cumulative
basis, that Colossians could not be by Paul.

What Bujard's case lacked was a thorough grounding in
statistics, by which alone one may judge how significant is a
result that shows deviation from a Pauline 'norm'. He also
failed to use any comparison outside the Pauline corpus
which might give a better sense of *how far* Colossians devi-
ated from the assured letters. Already in the 1960s
computers were beginning to come into use for stylistic
analysis (the technique was pioneered by A.Q. Morton) and

since then a highly sophisticated statistical method has developed in conjunction with computer technology, and is now employed in literary analysis in a number of disciplines. Sometimes, at least, such computer analyses really work. Recently, for instance, a book published anonymously in America under the title *Primary Colours* was compared by computer analysis to the style of a number of possible authors (political journalists) and shown to be closest to that of Joe Klein (a columnist for *Newsweek*). He initially denied authorship, but was later forced by supplementary handwriting analysis to admit that the computer had pointed in the right direction all along. Thus we might hope that if we could run the right tests through a computer, the mystery of Colossians would be solved once and for all.

There have been a number of recent attempts to determine the authentic Pauline letters along these lines, most notably in the books by A. Kenny and K. Neumann and in some articles by D. Mealand. Unfortunately, they come to different conclusions, or at least finish with different degrees of certainty. Kenny cautiously concluded that he saw 'no reason to reject the hypothesis that twelve of the Pauline Epistles are the work of an unusually versatile author' (p. 100). Neumann found the disputed letters (Ephesians and Colossians) closer to the Pauline norm than the Pastorals or other New Testament writers, while Mealand reported good evidence for the distinctiveness of Colossians and Ephesians as compared to the seven assured letters. Thus, just as it seemed as if a truly objective basis for decision was being discovered, different experts give us different verdicts.

For those (like me) who are not trained in statistics or in the technicalities of computer literary analyses, it is very hard to understand, let alone to assess, the workings and the arguments of these experts. However, it is clear that there are a number of difficulties with this sort of analysis, which will always render its verdicts somewhat problematical. For instance:

1. It is not always agreed by the experts what are the best tests of 'style'. To achieve results that are statistically significant requires measuring something that occurs

frequently (e.g. use of words that begin with a certain letter, or the position of the subject in the sentence), but it is debatable which are the most valuable definers of style. Some older forms of test, for example concerning sentence length, have now been thoroughly discredited.

2. Clearly it is better to run a range of tests rather than just one or two, in the hope that patterns will emerge (a 'multivariate' approach uses several variables at once). But how does one assess the situation if different tests bring different results? There is a danger here of in-built bias in highlighting only those tests that show *difference* and discounting those that prove unable to discriminate.

3. Some would question whether our samples of literature are big enough or representative enough to be amenable to proper testing. Some New Testament experts work with 750-word samples, others with 1000 words, but are even the latter big enough? Moreover, in the case of Colossians, some scholars would argue that considerable sections of the letter are based on pre-formed hymnic or ethical traditions, and so do not reveal the author's own hand. On this basis, for instance, Mealand's sample begins after 1.15-20, but it has been argued (e.g. by Cannon) that large parts of the rest of the letter are also heavily dependent on tradition. Even if they are not tradition-based, should we make allowances for authors' variations in style according to the genre in which they write or their subject matter? In other words, are we being careful enough to compare like with like?

4. The most difficult question is to assess how great a stylistic difference has to be before we are forced to recognize the work of a different author. Neumann helpfully compared a range of New Testament authors, and found the disputed letters closer to Paul than to others, but that is only what one would expect from a skilful imitator. Mealand presents a range of graphs showing the relative distances of Pauline and other writings from each other, but it is extremely hard to assess what the distances represent, especially as they vary from one graph to another. In the case of the book *Primary Colours* mentioned above, the computer was able to compare the unknown author with a range of *known* authors and thus see who was closest. But in the case of Colossians,

we are positing an *unknown* author, whose style is not otherwise available to us. We can judge that Colossians is a little unlike Paul in certain respects, but not that it is like any 'Paulinist' whom we know independently.

5. Indeed, our greatest difficulty in this case is that, if Colossians is pseudonymous, it is the work of a very careful *imitator* of Paul. Stylistic tests can obviously work well in discriminating between two different authors writing in their own style, but they have a much harder task in distinguishing between an original author and someone else who is steeped in his language and thought. To use a musical parallel, it is known that Mozart did not finish his Requiem Mass (K.626) before he died, and that it was finished off by his pupil Süssmayr. Mozart had discussed the unfinished parts of the work and sketched out some elements of them, but it is now often impossible to tell what in the later sections is Mozart's own work and what that of Süssmayr. One meets things which it seems Mozart would never have accepted, followed immediately by some entirely Mozartian passage. If Colossians was written by such a careful pupil and imitator of Paul, will we ever be able to say for sure from whose hand it comes?

Thus, as Mealand himself acknowledges, 'at the end of the day statistics does not provide a magical black box' (p. 79); indeed, sceptics will recall the cynical saying about 'lies, damned lies and statistics'! The results of these statistical analyses will depend to a degree on the ways the material is fed in, and the presuppositions with which the statistics are read. They confirm the presence of stylistic difference, and thus suggest the possibility of another author, without being able to provide decisive proof.

Conclusions (or Anti-Conclusions)

For many contemporary scholars the stylistic evidence is strong enough on its own to rule out Pauline authorship, though the difficulties noted above might cause some to modify their confidence a little. For others, the combination of the theological and stylistic differences makes the case on

a cumulative basis. Some such accumulation is certainly
legitimate (so long as only strong arguments are included,
and not the weak as well), and those who defend Pauline
authorship would be well advised to meet the force of the
whole cumulative argument and not to attempt to win the
day by piecemeal counter-arguments. The force of tradition
and non-academic factors must also be acknowledged on both
sides. 'Conservative' positions may be influenced by church
expectations, or the ethos of the institution in which such
scholars work or the publisher for whom they write: to
concede Colossians would certainly necessitate the 'fall' of
Ephesians and the Pastorals as well. On the other side,
hidden factors may require a reconstruction of Paul's image
free of the complications or disappointments of Colossians,
and the growing custom of discussing Pauline theology by
reference only to the seven 'assured' letters makes Colossians
look odd simply because it is always omitted from that
discussion.

And now we may add one further complication. We noted
above that the arguments about historical plausibility did
not point strongly towards a date later than Paul's lifetime.
Could the stylistic, and perhaps also the theological, differences between Colossians and other Pauline letters be put
down to the use of a secretary or an associate in the composition of this letter? We know that Paul did use secretaries
(e.g. Tertius, Rom. 16.23), and secretaries could be used in a
great variety of ways, ranging from mere dictation to co-
authorship or independent composition (see Richards). Has
Paul relied more on a secretary here than in other letters?
That is a possibility one could neither prove nor rule out,
though one might ask why he would do so in this case, and
how likely it is that he would give a secretary this degree of
freedom in moulding the theology of the letter. Alternatively,
could he have entrusted the composition of this letter to an
associate? This theory has been advanced by a few scholars
(e.g. Schweizer's commentary, pp. 15-24) and usually takes
Timothy, named in the opening salutation (1.1), as the most
likely candidate. It is in fact somewhat doubtful that
Timothy, who according to Acts 16.1-3 was uncircumcised
until adulthood, would have written disparagingly about

uncircumcision in the terms of 2.13. But more generally, the
question again arises whether Paul would have allowed an
associate to write a letter in his name which included such
differences from his own theology. This solution (which
appeals also to Dunn) thus looks neat, but it depends on
unknown and imponderable factors; to many it appears too
'convenient' by half.

Thus we are faced with an interesting conundrum that
shows how difficult it is to draw neat lines around authors
and their thought. Scholars are notoriously unwilling to
admit ignorance or indecision [the Latin for 'we do not know'
is 'ignoramus'!], but it is not the object of this guide to give
'answers', only to indicate by what means readers might
assess the matter for themselves. If the decision proves to be
a close call, or even impossible, that might cause us to reflect
a little more on authorship and individuality. It turns out, for
example, that the differences are not large between Paul
himself writing this letter, Paul writing with the aid of a
secretary, Paul authorizing an associate to write it, and the
letter being composed by a knowledgeable imitator or pupil
of Paul. Perhaps with our intense concern to demarcate
'Paul' from 'non-Paul' we are working with an artificial or
anachronistic notion of individual uniqueness: was Paul
completely different from his contemporaries and associates,
or did he typically work with others, influencing them and
being influenced by them? Have we created a Paul of utter
uniqueness in line with the peculiarly modern cult of the
individual? Whether by Paul, by a secretary, by an associate
or by a pupil, Colossians is clearly a 'Pauline' letter. Readers
must decide for themselves whether they can place it more
precisely than that, and if so where.

Further Reading

All commentaries include a discussion of this issue in an introduction or
excursus. In addition, see the following literature, mostly cited in this
chapter:

Baur, F.C., *Paul, the Apostle of Jesus Christ* (trans. A. Menzies from 2nd
    edn; 2 vols.; London/Edinburgh: Williams & Norgate, 1875 [1845]).

Bujard, W., *Stilanalytische Untersuchungen zum Kolosserbrief als Beitrag zur Methodik von Sprachvergleichen* (Göttingen: Vandenhoeck & Ruprecht, 1973).

Bultmann, R., *Theology of the New Testament* (trans. K. Grobel; 2 vols.; London: SCM Press, 1955), pp. 175-80.

Cannon, G.E., *The Use of Traditional Materials in Colossians* (Macon, GA: Mercer University Press, 1983).

Chadwick, H., ' "All Things to All Men" (1 Cor. ix.22)', NTS 1 (1954–55), pp. 261-75.

Käsemann, E., 'A Primitive Christian Baptismal Liturgy', in *Essays on New Testament Themes* (trans. W.J. Montague; London: SCM Press, 1964), pp. 149-68.

Kenny, A., *A Stylometric Study of the New Testament* (Oxford: Clarendon Press, 1986).

Kiley, M., *Colossians as Pseudepigraphy* (BibSem, 4; Sheffield: JSOT Press, 1986).

Kümmel, W.G., *Introduction to the New Testament* (trans. A.J. Mattill; London: SCM Press, 1966).

MacDonald, M., *The Pauline Churches: A Socio-Historical Study of Institutionalization in the Pauline and Deutero-Pauline Writings* (Cambridge: Cambridge University Press, 1988).

Marxsen, W., *Introduction to the New Testament* (trans. G. Buswell; Oxford: Blackwell, 1968).

Meade, D.G., *Pseudonymity and Canon* (Grand Rapids: Eerdmans, 1987).

Mealand, D.L., 'The Extent of the Pauline Corpus: A Multivariate Approach', *JSNT* 59 (1995), pp. 61-92.

Neumann, K.J., *The Authenticity of the Pauline Epistles in the Light of Stylostatistical Analysis* (Atlanta: Scholars Press, 1990).

Richards, E.R., *The Secretary in the Letters of Paul* (Tübingen: Mohr [Paul Siebeck], 1991).

Sanders, E.P., 'Literary Dependence in Colossians', *JBL* 85 (1966), pp. 28-45.

Schenk, W., 'Der Kolosserbrief in der neueren Forschung (1945–1985)', *ANRW*, II.25.4, pp. 3327-64.

3

THE TARGET OF COLOSSIANS

A Letter with a Target

Every letter has a purpose. One may write to console, to inform, to encourage, to congratulate—indeed for any purpose imaginable—so it is reasonable to ask what the author of Colossians was writing for. The letter opens in a friendly and encouraging tone, but in 2.8 a note of warning is introduced, and the rest of that chapter is full of barbed remarks about some 'philosophy' and 'empty deceit' (2.8). Thus, at least in part, the letter is targeted against something or someone; as so often in the New Testament we are witnessing a fight. It is not entirely clear whether the author has his sights on that target throughout the letter or only where it is overtly mentioned. Is the material in ch. 1, for instance, a quite innocent exposition of the gospel and the cosmic role of Christ, or is it designed to stockpile the theological weapons necessary for the attack in ch. 2? The way in which the opening salvo in 2.8 leads into comments on Christ's 'fulness' (2.8-9; cf. 1.15-20) strongly suggests the latter option, but it is less clear how the material in chs. 3 and 4 relates to the battle played out in ch. 2. As we shall see, judging where and how to 'mirror-read' this letter, reconstructing its target from the direction and nature of its attack, proves to be an uncommonly difficult task.

New Testament scholars love polemics, and they are attracted to this letter by the sound of gunfire. We should, however, be wary lest we exaggerate the extent of the battle, or 'discover' polemical nuances in the letter where none exist.

Compared to the letter to the Galatians, which starts fizzing from its very first phrase, Colossians is written in a rather calmer tone. On that basis Morna Hooker argued that our author considered the threat to the Colossians remote; he was content to issue a general warning, and did not have a specific 'error' in view. That, however, seems to exaggerate in the other direction. If the letter lacks some of Paul's fury, that could be because it is not by Paul anyway (see above, Chapter 2), and there is enough in the pointed rebuke and sarcasm of 2.16-23 to indicate that our author felt the threat he warned against to be real, immediate and specific. Thus we are entitled to ask what the letter was directed against and are initially encouraged to hope that we might be able to draw quite a sharp profile of that target.

In recent scholarship on Colossians, a huge amount of effort has been invested in the attempt to draw that profile. This is not merely out of historical curiosity or the need to find a knotty problem for a PhD thesis. Most New Testament scholars have assumed that to comprehend this letter we need to understand what it is combatting: if it is such a responsive and 'occasional' letter, we need to know what occasioned it. Literary theory would question that assumption, affirming that the meaning of a text is not dependent on knowing its historical origins and purposes. Nonetheless, historians are entitled to make a modest claim, that a text situated so specifically in a historical occasion will be more fully comprehended if we appreciate its contemporary historical context. Colossians can communicate and has communicated through the centuries to those who know nothing of its original context; but historians can attempt to offer a richer appreciation of the force and texture of its message by reconstructing the struggle in which it engages. Whether in this case their attempt can succeed is another matter.

But there is another reason why the search for the target of Colossians has been, and continues to be, so intense. Since the early nineteenth century, New Testament scholarship has been fascinated by the diversity in early Christianity, and has found intra-mural Christian polemic to be a valuable window onto that diversity. Thus, ironically, letters like this which were designed to warn against 'perversions' of

Christianity, precisely bring such alternatives to the attention of the historian, who is eager to trace that process by which early Christianity defined its identity, limiting its options and drawing its boundaries against 'error'. Colossians thus promises to show us one example of that process, which we may compare and contrast with others found in the New Testament or in other early Christian documents. Since they typically sympathize with the viewpoint of the letter, most scholars refer to the alternative combatted here as heresy or false teaching. A more neutral historical stance would avoid such loaded terms or insist on placing them in inverted commas, since the labels 'orthodoxy' and 'heresy' represent value judgments about truth. The line of thought in 2.18-19 ('let no-one disqualify you...not holding fast to the Head') strongly suggests that the author's targets are Christians, whom he considers to be lapsing through their 'empty deceit'. But it is possible that this alternative form of Christianity had more to commend it than our author allows. Unfortunately, our only access to it is through the polemic of Colossians, which one may suspect of hostile selectivity and caricature.

The Range of Reconstructions on Offer

In the course of 2.8-23 the author of Colossians attacks a 'philosophy' which is 'according to human tradition, according to the elemental spirits (or simply, elements) of the universe' (2.8), with which he contrasts the fulness of Christ (2.9-10). He refers to a Christian kind of 'circumcision' (2.11-12) and celebrates the death and resurrection of Christ, by which 'the rulers and authorities' were defeated (2.13-15). He resists a tendency to judge 'in matters of food or drink, or of observing festivals, new moons, or sabbaths' (2.16) and refutes attempts to 'disqualify' which require 'self-abasement' and the 'worship of angels' (2.18). Referring again to 'the elements/elemental spirits of the universe' (2.20), he lambasts regulations such as 'Do not handle, do not taste, do not touch' (2.20-21) which seem to promote 'wisdom' and 'piety' and 'severe treatment of the body', but are, in his view, wholly counter-productive (2.22-23).

Such are the chief elements of this section of polemic (using the NRSV translation; 2.18 and 23 in fact abound with translation problems). They no doubt made good sense to the original recipients of this letter, but they are apt to bewilder us who read their correspondence two millennia later. The letter seems to scatter clues in our path but of such a fragmentary and disparate nature that scholar-detectives are clearly going to have a challenging job in piecing them together. The last 170 years have seen countless attempts to solve this puzzle, but none have won more than partial or temporary assent. Whereas there is more or less settled consensus about the target of Paul's attack in Galatians or the viewpoints Paul combats in 1 Corinthians, here there is not only no consensus but, it seems, an ever-increasing diversity in the range of reconstructions on offer. The less consensus there is, the more tempting it is for scholars to try 'one more time' to crack this puzzle. But the greater the variety of solutions, the more baffled are the observers of this game who wonder what is wrong when the same clues can lead in such disparate directions! Are Colossian scholars exceptionally obtuse, or are the clues simply too sparse or too obscure to lead us to any solution at all?

It would be tedious to attempt to survey here all the solutions that have been offered; it is also unnecessary, since the student may readily find such a survey in the introductions to the commentaries, or, at greater length, in the monographs by Francis and Meeks and DeMaris (see Further Reading; subsequent to DeMaris are the newest solutions offered by Dunn, Arnold and Martin). It may be helpful, however, to outline some of the most important trends in the history of this investigation so as to gain some orientation in what is otherwise a baffling mass of conflicting theories. We may distinguish five main schools of thought.

1. *Lightfoot and Bornkamm: Jewish-Christian Gnosticism.* J.B. Lightfoot, arguably the greatest British biblical scholar of the nineteenth century (1828–89), offered a pioneering reconstruction of the Colossian 'heresy' in the introduction to his commentary on the letter (reprinted in Francis and Meeks, pp. 13-59). Since he held to the Pauline authorship of Colossians, it was important for him to counter radical

German theories that it was a pseudonymous letter directed against a form of Gnosticism only evidenced after Paul's lifetime. The Jewish features of the 'heresy' were self-evident to Lightfoot: the references to circumcision, sabbaths and new moons, and the rules about food and drink all pointed in that direction. But it was also clear that there were elements in this 'heresy' that were 'alien to the spirit of Judaism proper', most notably: (1) its concern with wisdom, knowledge and mystery (Lightfoot took the author's use of such themes to signal their importance in his target); (2) its fascination with angels and other intermediary 'powers'; and (3) its interest in asceticism and humiliation of the body. Lightfoot considered that there was, in fact, a close parallel to this amalgam in a form of Judaism contemporary to Paul, that is, the Judaism espoused by the Essenes. Since he was writing before the discovery of the Dead Sea Scrolls (which most scholars consider to be related to the Essenes), Lightfoot had to rely on the somewhat partial representations of the Essenes provided by Josephus and Philo; but he found there the same interest in angels, in ascetic practices and in knowledge which he considered distinctive in the type of Judaism influential in the Colossian church. By a somewhat loose employment of the term 'Gnostic', Lightfoot was able to dub the Essenes a form of pre-Christian Judaic Gnosticism, and without claiming precisely that the Colossian 'heresy' originated in Essenism, he thought he had detected 'an essential affinity of type'. Scraps of evidence about Jews in Asia suggested that they did not necessarily belong to 'the normal Pharisaic type'; they thus provided the potential setting for a Jewish-Christian Gnosticism that was later to take more definite shape in the teaching of Cerinthus, a Gnostic Christian at the end of the first century.

It was to be sometime after Lightfoot's death before the 'Gnostic' aspect of his hypothesis was given sharper definition. Gnosticism was to fascinate a whole generation of German New Testament scholars from the 1920s to the 1950s: for Bousset, Bultmann and their pupils it provided the key to understanding the background and context of early Christianity. It was one of Bultmann's pupils, Günther Bornkamm, who in 1948 wrote an influential essay on 'The

Heresy of Colossians' (translated in Francis and Meeks, pp. 123-45). Bornkamm takes as his starting-point the references in the letter to the 'elements/elemental spirits of the universe' (Greek, *stoicheia tou kosmou*, 2.8, 20), which he connects with the references to 'powers' in 2.10 and 2.15, the mention of angels in 2.18, and the talk of 'fullness' (Greek, *plērōma*) in 2.9. For Bornkamm, this indicates that the 'heretical doctrine' advocated worship of personal angelic or astral powers, which required the observance of festivals and seasons and demanded certain ascetic practices. Since this is a Christian 'error', these elemental powers must have been somehow related to Christ, who was perhaps understood to have embodied their fullness. These individual traits 'extracted and inferred from the statements of Colossians' can then be correlated with the evidence for 'ancient mythology and speculation of the Oriental Aeon-theology, which was widespread and active in Hellenistic syncretism' (p. 126). Drawing parallels with a reconstructed Mithras liturgy, Bornkamm suggests that the Colossian 'error' celebrated a mystery of rebirth with a Gnostic flavour (e.g. in ascetic 'stripping off of the body'). The Jewish elements in the 'heresy' suggest that this was a Jewish Gnosticism, but one whose syncretism has fundamentally altered the shape and meaning of the Jewish practices mentioned (feasts, fasts, circumcision, food laws). The 'syncretistic' conditions of Diaspora Judaism make this entirely plausible, and Bornkamm points to the later 'Hypsistarians' as a successor in Asian Christianity to the Jewish-Christian Gnosticism combatted in Colossians.

The Lightfoot–Bornkamm solution has been refined and modified in minor ways over the years, but its basic shape remains an influential option, especially in German scholarship, where first-century 'Gnosticism' is discussed with more confidence than elsewhere (see also Knox and Goulder). Bornkamm, it will be noticed, dropped Lightfoot's parallel with the Essenes. Discoveries at Qumran have (probably) given us much fuller information about the Essenes, and have encouraged further drawing of parallels between the Colossian target and the Dead Sea sect. But these are now less frequently discussed under the rubric of 'Gnosticism', and we will encounter them in a different kind of hypothesis below (section 3).

2. *Dibelius: A Christianized Mystery Cult.* Martin Dibelius (1883–1947) was one of the principal scholars within the 'History of Religions School' that flourished in Germany either side of the turn of the twentieth century and produced pioneering explorations of the parallels between early Christianity and its social and religious environment. At the age of 34 Dibelius wrote an extraordinarily learned essay on initiatory rites (translated in Francis and Meeks, pp. 61-121), which argued that Colossians was directed against Christians who had adapted a pagan mystery cult, dedicated to 'the elements of the world'. Dibelius takes it as uncontroversial that Christians in Colossae were beginning to worship 'the elements' and adopting ascetic practices to suit, but his eye is drawn particularly to 2.18 whose language of 'mortification', 'angels' (= the elements) and 'entering' he considered to be technical terms in the 'heretical teaching', here echoed by the author. At this point we need to note a difficult Greek phrase in 2.18 which was crucial to Dibelius's hypothesis. After talking about 'the worship of angels' (to which we will return below), the author of Colossians wrote a puzzling phrase, *ha heoraken embateuōn*, which may mean something like 'which he has seen entering' (NRSV translates 'dwelling on visions'; REB, 'access to some visionary world'). Dibelius was struck by the fact that the rare verb *embateuō* had recently been found in some (second century CE) inscriptions from the temple of Apollo at Claros (in the province of Asia), where it seemed to relate to an entry-rite associated with initiation into the mystery of Apollo. He considered that the peculiar phrase in Col. 2.18 alludes to the practice of entering (in an initiation) into that which the initiate saw (in preparatory visions), and he connected this with one of the few glimpses we have of mystery initiations in antiquity, the description of Isis-initiation in Apuleius, *Metamorphoses* 11. There Lucius, the hero, in preparation for his initiation is taken symbolically through the elements of the universe—providing for Dibelius a link with the phrase in Col. 2.8, 20.

This ingenious piecing together of the puzzle had one serious weakness: it placed the Colossian 'heresy' within the framework of contemporary pagan practice, but could not easily explain those elements in the letter that seemed to be of Jewish origin. Dibelius in fact denied that there was anything in the letter that suggested a Jewish tinge to the 'heresy': 'angels' can be talked of by non-Jews; the calendrical observances relate to reverence for the stars, not Judaism; and the circumcision language is the author's own, not part of the 'heresy'. For Dibelius, no thesis of 'syncretistic' Asian Judaism is called for. Rather, we have a fine example of 'the syncretization of Christianity' in which early mystical forms of gnosis (not yet a developed Gnosticism) proved attractive to Christians as a kind of secondary religious insurance. Dibelius thus finds in Paul's struggle with this 'error' (he takes the letter as authentic) evidence from the first generation of Christianity for the titanic struggle between Christian exclusiveness and the syncretistic spirit of the age. Even if one disagrees with his thesis, the final pages of Dibelius's article are well worth reading for his exposition of this struggle.

3. *Francis: Mystical Jewish Ascent.* A major new alternative was opened up in scholarship by an article published by Fred Francis in 1963 (reprinted in Francis and Meeks, pp. 163-95). Like Dibelius, Francis took the interpretation of 2.18 to be crucial, but what he found here was very different. The reference to 'self-mortification' (Greek, *tapeinophrosunē*) he regarded as a technical term for fasting, and its association with the visions suggested some mystical experience effected by a fasting regime. But this he found to be common not only in the Hellenistic world generally but also, and especially, in Jewish post-biblical literature. Here Francis made use of Gershom Scholem's pioneering research on Jewish mysticism, which placed on the scholarly map in the postwar period the phenomenon of Jewish asceticism and mystical ascent, experiences which were often accompanied by visions and a sense of entering one of the heavens (cf. 2 Cor. 12.1-6). But what about the reference in Col. 2.18 to 'the worship of angels'? Up till this point nearly all scholars had taken this phrase (Greek, *thrēskeia tōn angellōn*) to mean 'worship directed to angels' and had considered the 'heresy' to involve some rather un-Jewish practice of veneration of

angels/elements/powers. Francis, however, argued that the phrase could be translated as a subjective genitive: not worship directed to angels, but worship practised by angels. If this is the case, then the 'heresy' could involve fascination with, or even human participation in, the heavenly angelic worship of God, an activity commented on in Jewish apocalyptic and other 'visionary' literature.

This mode of reconstruction prefers talk of 'mysticism' to that of 'Gnosticism' and regards the 'error' in Colossae as explicable within an entirely Jewish framework of thought and practice. It thus serves as a mirror-image of the reconstruction offered by Dibelius, maximizing the Jewish features of the 'error' which he had dismissed, and dismissing the 'pagan' worship of 'powers' or 'elements' which he had taken to be foundational. This reconstruction has fitted very well the post-war mood in New Testament scholarship in which the Jewish background to early Christianity has been re-emphasized, not least because of the discovery of the Dead Sea Scrolls, where interest in knowledge, angels and participation in heavenly worship has suggested many parallels with the Colossian 'error' (e.g. Lyonnet's essay translated in Francis and Meeks, pp. 147-61). Jewish apocalypticism has been extensively explored as a plausible framework for the Colossian 'error' (Rowland and Sappington), while current fascination with 'the parting of the ways' between early Christianity and Judaism has encouraged scholars to take the Colossian combat as a phenomenon not unlike what we find in Galatians (e.g. Wright and Dunn). On this basis, scholars can make a general appeal to the presence and importance of Jews in Asia Minor to support this thesis of a (mystical) Judaism as an attraction to early Christian converts, while dismissing parallels with 'mystery cults' and 'Gnosticism' that are now regarded in English-speaking scholarship as offering no valid analogy with early Christianity.

4. *Schweizer, DeMaris and Martin: Hellenistic Philosophy.* A quite different interpretative tack has been taken more recently by some scholars who find the appropriate 'background' to the Colossian 'heresy' in some branch of Hellenistic philosophy. These scholars take the letter's reference

to the target as a 'philosophy' (2.8; NRSV, 'speculations') as a straightforward descriptor, and are responsive to a widespread 'rediscovery' of Hellenism, particularly Hellenistic popular philosophy, among contemporary New Testament scholars. In his commentary on Colossians (1976), Eduard Schweizer pioneered this development, being particularly impressed by the author's repetition of the phrase 'the elements of the world' (2.8, 20). Schweizer took this phrase to refer not to spirits or astral powers but to the (four) physical elements of the world, which were regarded by some Greek philosophers as being in constant strife and as holding humanity captive in the physical world. Schweizer took the 'self-mortification' of the 'heretics' to concern fasting and sexual abstinence, enforced by rules about food, drink and festivals which had only a superficially Jewish character. Moreover, he considered he had found a perfect parallel to all these elements in a neo-Pythagorean text from the first century (preserved in Diogenes Laertius, *Lives* 8.25-33). Thus the 'heresy' was a slightly Judaized Pythagoreanism, which added to belief in Christ the worship of angels and the goal of the soul's ascent, through asceticism, to the upper world.

A different philosophical background has been suggested by Richard DeMaris. Doubting Schweizer's supposed Pythagorean parallel, DeMaris posits a syncretistic philosophy which has elements of Middle-Platonic demonology together with a Jewish-Christian emphasis on humility, food and calendrical requirements; these are truly Jewish, but their observance is no longer motivated by purely Jewish concerns. DeMaris insists that the controversial phrase 'the worship of angels' (2.18) means that angels are themselves worshipped (*contra* Francis), though the 'angels' in this case are another name for pagan heroes or lesser divinities; in any case, this clearly shows that the 'heresy' goes beyond Judaism. The term *embateuō* in the same verse should, he argues, be given the sense of 'investigate', and this signals the philosophical tone of the 'heresy' which attracted Christians precisely by its combination of Jewish tradition and Greek philosophy.

Troy Martin, on the other hand, argues that Cynic philosophers have penetrated the Colossian congregation, criticizing its practices and advocating an ascetic Cynic lifestyle. Martin's starting-point is the discussion about abstinence in 2.20-23, which he takes to indicate distinctively Cynic prohibitions of perishable 'consumer goods', and an understanding of 'humility' as bodily discipline, not social respect. He then offers a novel reading of 2.16-18 whose contents he takes to reveal not the practices of the philosophers but the characteristics of the Colossian Christians, which are coming under Cynic criticism. Thus he reads 2.16 as 'Let no one critique you for your eating and drinking, or your observance of feasts, new moons and sabbaths.' The author of Colossians himself supports the practices listed here (the celebration of the Eucharist and the observance of a Jewish calendar) against Cynic criticism of their artificiality. The contentious phrase *thrēskeia tōn angellōn* (2.18) does not mean worship of angels or worship with them: the genitive is of *source* and the phrase means 'the religion communicated by human messengers' (those who preached the gospel in Colossae), another ground on which the Cynics criticize the Colossian Christians.

5. *Arnold: Syncretistic Folk Religion.* Clinton Arnold's is one of the most recent configurations of the Colossian 'philosophy' (1995); it bears some similarities to previous solutions (e.g. Dibelius and Lähnemann), but is distinguished by its emphasis on local popular religion, especially the use of magic and the invocation of 'angels' to ward off malevolent powers. Dismissing 'Gnosticism' as a later and esoteric development, Arnold argues that *thrēskeia tōn angellōn* (2.18) must mean veneration of angels and has nothing to do with Jewish mysticism. In a thorough survey of magical papyri and of inscriptions from Asia Minor, Arnold highlights the common appeal to 'angels' by both Jews and Gentiles, and notes the 'syncretistic' atmosphere that such anxious invocations and incantations betray at the level of ordinary 'folk' piety. Like Dibelius he finds in 2.18 the technical language of mystery initiation, but he does not deny the simultaneous influence of Judaism, as evidenced both by the Jewish rites mentioned in 2.16 and by Jewish interest in magic and angels. In the syncretistic atmosphere of Phrygia and Lydia an amalgam of Jewish and pagan religiosity has further

combined with Christian beliefs in a common concern to avert the influences of the 'powers' and (personal) 'elements'. Arnold's thesis exemplifies a recent revival of interest in magic (including Jewish magic) as a key element in popular religion, and he renews Dibelius's fascination with the development of early Christianity in a highly syncretistic age. By his careful research of local primary sources which could explain the specificity of the Colossian 'heresy', and by avoiding some of the more obvious weaknesses of other hypotheses, his thesis looks set to have a considerable impact on scholarship.

Some Questions of Method

Scholars who survey this mass of hypothetical reconstructions are apt to be dismayed by the failure of the guild to reach unanimity on even the rudiments of a solution; students may be excused for being baffled or distinctly unimpressed. The fact that the main schools of thought outlined above have spawned multiple permutations and hybrids only adds to the impression that this is an arbitrary scholarly game in which one admits or dismisses 'evidence' without methodological control and fits it into whatever framework one likes (Gnosticism, mystery cult, philosophy, apocalyptic Judaism etc.). I have suggested above that the variations in solution do, to some extent, follow scholarly fashions in emphasizing different aspects of the cultural and religious context of early Christianity, with scholars naturally drawn towards hypotheses that fit their own expertise or the current interests of their generation. In this regard, it is revealing to watch what scholars describe as their 'clear' or 'uncontroversial' starting-points. As we have seen, for some the Jewish character of the 'error' is clear from the references to circumcision, new moons and sabbaths; for others these are merely surface phenomena to be fitted into some predominantly non-Jewish philosophy or mystery. For some scholars, the essential feature of the 'heresy' was its interest in 'philosophy' or its fascination with 'the elements/elementary spirits of the universe'; for others, such language tells us more about *the author's interpretation* of the 'heresy' than about the 'heresy' itself. Thus scholars construct their hypotheses on entirely different foundations, often unaware that what they take for granted has not seemed to others at all self-evident. Beyond that point, as we have seen, they fit 'asceticism' and food rules into the picture in a wide variety of ways and offer hugely variant translations of key phrases in 2.18, whose reference to 'the worship of angels' has proved to be the watershed from which interpretations stream in quite opposite directions. Just to compound the problem, scholars are apt to use terms like 'Gnosticism', 'apocalyptic', 'syncretism' and 'mysticism' somewhat vaguely, and even understandings of what is 'Jewish' (or 'Essene') have varied over time. Almost everyone can claim to have found some parallel to their reconstruction of the 'heresy' in the diverse religious environment of Asia Minor!

If this scholarly game is not to become wearisome or entirely ludicrous, it clearly requires some methodological rigour. I have elsewhere suggested some controls in this business of 'mirror-reading' a polemical letter (see Barclay in Further Reading, together with the book by Sumney), but it may be helpful to highlight here three questions of method which readers may find handy as critical tools when assessing scholars' attempts to reconstruct the target of Colossians:

1. *Where Can we Trace the Target?* As we noted at the outset, the letter to the Colossians does not give the appearance of fighting at every turn, yet there are some passages outside ch. 2 which can be plausibly connected to the main battle-ground delineated there. As a matter of principle, it seems best to insist that one's starting point should always be within 2.8-23, the overtly polemical passage; other parts of the letter should only be brought into the picture if they are clearly related, verbally or thematically, to the battle-lines drawn in ch. 2. However, even within 2.8-23 there are some uncertainties about the *immediacy* of the attack on the target. The specific lines of argumentation in 2.16-23 are clear enough, but what inferences should we draw from the more general depiction of baptism and salvation in 2.11-15? Does this suggest that the 'heresy' also had an initiatory rite like baptism? Or does our author's use of the metaphor of

circumcision suggest that the 'heretics' also practised a (more
literal) form of circumcision? Since this is, at most, an indirect allusion to the 'heresy', it seems safest to regard these
verses as less reliable evidence than the direct offensive
launched in 2.16-23.

2. *Whose Line Is it Anyway?* Even when we have identified
where the attack is direct, we still have to judge how much it
reveals. If a politician attacks his or her opponents as 'a
bunch of crooks', we are not likely to consult police records in
order to identify them: we know this is a general piece of
abuse that tells us nothing about the character of the opponents. Even if we hear them attacked as, say, 'Marxists' or
'fascists', we are (most of us) sensible enough to take those as
political caricatures that reveal practically nothing of the
opponents' stance. In this regard, New Testament scholars
seem remarkably naive when it comes to the polemic in
Colossians (perhaps due to a reluctance to admit that it
might be nasty enough to caricature its opponents). When
our author introduces his attack with a warning against
'empty deceit' (2.8), we know to ignore that as invective; but
why should we take any more seriously the claim that the
'error' is 'according to human tradition'? (Schweizer took that
to prove that the festivals and fasts had a secular, not a religious, origin.) More seriously, does the author cite the
disqualifications and rules in 2.16, 18 and 21 accurately and
fully, or are these a loaded and caricatured selection? For
instance, in that phrase 'the worship of angels' (2.18), which
has caused so much trouble to interpreters, are we hearing
the language and thought of the 'heresy' clearly and directly,
or is this a polemical and one-sided representation of a practice that the 'heretics' might have described rather differently? Clearly, it must be close enough to 'reality' for the
recipients of this letter to recognize what the author is referring to, but we are familiar enough with the loaded ways in
which Protestants have accused Catholics of 'worshipping
Mary' to know that, for instance, a fascination with angels as
mediators of prayers and blessings could be polemically
twisted as 'the worship of angels'. It is curious how, in their
debates on whether the genitive in that phrase is to be taken
as objective (worship directed to angels) or subjective

(worship conducted by angels), scholars have rarely stopped to ask whether what they are reading is, in any case, straight reportage.

This issue of whose language we are hearing is crucial in some other cases too. How literally should we take the reference to 'philosophy' in 2.8? Is this a term used by the 'heretics' or by the author of Colossians? Since the term is not inherently polemical, and since the author suggests that the 'heresy' offers some form of 'wisdom' (2.23), we might be inclined to take 'philosophy' as part of the vocabulary of the 'heresy'. But we would still want to ask what was implied by this term. It does not necessarily entail what we think of as 'philosophy', since all kinds of intellectual and religious options were packaged as 'philosophies' in antiquity. Thus a promising starting-point does not get us as far as we might think! And what about the phrase used in both 2.8 and 2.20, 'the elements/elemental spirits of the universe'? As the alternative translations indicate, the Greek phrase used here, *ta stoicheia tou kosmou*, is open to a range of interpretations, and has been the topic of scholarly debate for decades. But whose terminology is this anyway? It is almost universally assumed by scholars that this phrase takes us straight to the language of the 'heresy', so that one may immediately debate what kind of 'elements' were meant and what sort of fear or veneration they elicited in the 'heresy'. But the alternative should be seriously considered (it was once argued very effectively by Ernst Percy): that *ta stoicheia tou kosmou* is a polemical phrase coined by our author (or borrowed from Gal. 4.3, 9), which *caricatures* the 'heresy' as enslavement to physical or cosmological 'elements' (e.g. in rules concerning things which may not be touched or eaten), but hardly reflects its own view of the matter, let alone its precise terminology. This is a prime case where we have to assess whether the clues we are following are those left by the 'heresy' itself or by the author's (polemical) representation of it.

3. *How Do the Pieces of the Puzzle Fit Together?* It is only when we have critically sifted the material in Colossians to decide what constitutes 'evidence' that we can ask our third question regarding the shape into which the pieces fit. Without a picture to guide you, you cannot initially tell

whether a blue jigsaw piece is sky or sea, and the really crit-ical moves in reconstructing the Colossian puzzle are deci-sions about the basic outline of the picture. The repetition of the term 'self-abasement' (Greek, *tapeinophrosunē*) in 2.18 and 2.23 (where NRSV translates 'humility') strongly suggests that this concept (if not this precise term) plays a part in the 'heresy'. But what does this represent? DeMaris, noting the Jewish-Christian currency of this term, regards it as evidence of a Jewish moral emphasis; others link it with the rules about abstinence in touch or taste (2.21) and find here a suggestion of self-mortification. And what do these rules suggest? Is there some far-reaching asceticism at work here, motivated by a disdain of the body or Cynic rejection of artificial human products, or is this a case of bodily control in preparation for mystical or magical practices, or are these simply Jewish, or some other cultural, taboos in matters of food and drink? We may wish to compare Colossians with how Paul responds to Jewish taboos in his letters, but if our author is not Paul (see Chapter 2) that comparison will be unreliable, since the author of Colossians might respond to the same phenomena as Paul in very different terms. In general, we may say that the hardest thing to get access to is the motivation and cultural-religious framework in which the various items which are attacked here originally fitted. It is not the business of our author to set out the motives and presuppositions of his target, just to snipe at whatever he thought was vulnerable. As we have seen, 2.18 has plenty of translational (and, in fact, textual) problems to make discerning its 'evidence' hugely problematic; subsequently placing that 'evidence' within a larger framework is a doubly difficult task: in what context and for what reasons might someone want to 'worship' so-called 'angels'—or join in the 'worship' of 'angels'?

Is the Puzzle Soluble?

The methodological problems we have just considered should cause even the most confident sleuth to hesitate. We are trying to trace a target that we can see only through the haze of a polemical tirade, leaving traces that are brief, often ambiguous and sometimes wholly obscure. Because of the difficulty of placing this letter in the history of early Christianity, we cannot easily connect this controversy with other battles we can view more clearly (as we can, for instance, in the case of Galatians). Perhaps we should simply admit—although New Testament scholars seem reluctant ever to do so—that this puzzle is insoluble.

If such an answer seems unduly negative, readers are at least entitled to pour a little of the acid of scepticism over supposed reconstructions that are methodologically naive or vastly over-confident. For what it is worth, I may suggest here my own extremely cautious outline of the target of Colossians, indicating at each point the limitations of what we may guess.

If one may set up a hierarchy of probabilities, ranging from 'certain' to 'possible' (cf. also Hartman), we may say at the outset that *nothing* in this matter is certain. There are a few matters I would consider *highly probable*, such as:

1. The 'heresy' involved observance of the main elements of the Jewish calendar and some features of the Jewish food laws (2.16). The context and purposes of these observances are, however, uncertain.

2. Some visionary experiences were claimed, in association with worship (2.18); but it is unclear how frequent a phenomenon this was and whether the worship was being directed to 'angels' or in association with them.

3. Some regulations were involved, to do with physical activities (touch, eating and drinking, 2.20-23), though we cannot tell how comprehensive these were, or what motivated them.

4. The 'heresy' claimed to offer some 'wisdom' (2.8, 23), though what this consisted of is beyond our grasp.

In the category of the *probable*, I would place the following:

1. The 'heresy' is being sponsored by Christians (that seems to be implied by the connection between 2.18 and 2.19), who are taking a superior attitude to those who do not follow their path (2.16, 18). But we do not know anything

about the social aspects of this phenomenon, that is, what sort of people were involved and what it implied for their social standing or aspirations.
2. The 'heresy' included veneration for a variety of 'powers', which might lie behind the reference to 'angels' in 2.18 and the emphatic talk about the powers in 1.15-20, 2.9-10 and 2.15. We cannot tell in what context this veneration took place, nor how it related to Christ. Nor can we discern the significance or relevance of the phrase 'the elements of the universe' (2.8, 20).

As for what is *possible*, one could say many features of the reconstructions outlined above fit that category, but can be placed no higher, since they generally lack the exclusionary power to enable them to assert that they are more likely to be correct than some alternative. Reconstructions that obliterate the Jewish element in the mixture seem to be most precarious (on the basis of my first 'highly probable'), while those (e.g. Wright) that argue *both* that the letter is by Paul *and* that it reacts to the same issues addressed in Galatians adopt the least likely option, since they cannot then explain why the polemic in Colossians is so different from that in Galatians.

The problem with the limited reconstruction offered above is that the elements listed as 'highly probable' or 'probable' lack any religious or cultural framework, and it is precisely at that point that scholars' opinions are so divergent (Gnosticism, apocalyptic or mystical Judaism, Hellenistic philosophy, or some syncretistic amalgam). We may simply have to accept that that is an unsolved, and insoluble, mystery, and redirect our attention to the content of the letter's response; while that too concerns a 'mystery' (2.2), at least we have in this case direct access to a body of evidence, the letter itself.

Further Reading

All the commentaries include some discussion of this matter either in the introduction or in an excursus. In addition, see:

Arnold, C.E., *The Colossian Syncretism: The Interface between Christianity and Folk Belief at Colossae* (Tübingen: Mohr [Paul Siebeck], 1995).

Barclay, J.M.G., 'Mirror-Reading a Polemical Letter: Galatians as a Test Case', *JSNT* 31 (1987), pp. 73-93.

DeMaris, R.E., *The Colossian Controversy: Wisdom in Dispute at Colossae* (JSNTSup, 96; Sheffield: JSOT Press, 1994).

Dunn, J.D.G., 'The Colossian Philosophy: A Confident Jewish Apologia', *Bib* 76 (1995), pp. 153-81.

Francis, F.O., and W.A. Meeks, *Conflict at Colossae* (Missoula: Scholars Press 1975). Contains essays by Lightfoot, Dibelius, Bornkamm, Lyonnet and Francis, as well as a valuable introduction and epilogue.

Goulder, M., 'Colossians and Barbelo', *NTS* 41 (1995), pp. 601-19.

Hartman, L., 'Humble and Confident: On the So-called Philosophers in Colossae', in D. Hellholm, H. Moxnes and T. Karlsen Seim (eds.), *Mighty Minorities?* (Oslo: Scandinavian University Press, 1995), pp. 25-39.

Hooker, M.D., 'Were There False Teachers in Colossae?', in B. Lindars and S.S. Smalley (eds.), *Christ and Spirit in the New Testament: Studies in Honour of C.F.D. Moule* (Cambridge: Cambridge University Press, 1973), pp. 315-31; repr. in M.D. Hooker, *From Adam to Christ: Essays on Paul* (Cambridge: Cambridge University Press, 1990), pp. 121-36.

Knox, W.L., *St Paul and the Church of the Gentiles* (Cambridge: Cambridge University Press, 1939), pp. 146-78.

Lähnemann, J., *Der Kolosserbrief: Komposition, Situation und Argumentation* (Gütersloh: Gütersloher Verlaghaus/Gerd Mohn, 1971).

Martin, T.W., *By Philosophy and Empty Deceit: Colossians as a Response to a Cynic Critique* (JSNTSup, 118; Sheffield: Sheffield Academic Press, 1996).

Percy, E., *Die Probleme der Kolosser- und Epheserbriefe* (Lund: G.W.K. Gleerup, 1946).

Rowland, C., 'Apocalyptic Visions and the Exaltation of Christ in the Letter to the Colossians', *JSNT* 19 (1983), pp. 73-83.

Sappington, T.J., *Revelation and Redemption at Colossae* (JSNTSup, 53; Sheffield: JSOT Press, 1991).

Sumney, J.L., *Identifying Paul's Opponents: The Question of Method in 2 Corinthians* (JSNTSup, 40; Sheffield: JSOT Press, 1990).

4

THE COLOSSIAN HYMN
AND HOUSEHOLD CODE

The Interest in Pre-Formed Traditions

The letter to the Colossians contains two passages of great
interest to scholars looking for fragments of traditional material embedded in the New Testament. These two passages
are 'the Colossian hymn' contained in 1.15-20 and the code of
household duties in 3.18–4.1. As we shall see, the first
passage is more likely to represent a pre-formed unit than
the second, but it is important to clarify at the outset why
this search for textual fossils should be so absorbing.

The main reason for the search is the desire to find out
about the earliest stages of Christianity. It is a cruel and
frustrating fact that we are very poorly informed about the
first twenty or thirty years of the Christian movement. It
began in the early 30s of the first century, but our earliest
primary sources are Paul's letters, none of which can be
dated before the late 40s; the earliest gospel, Mark, was
written no earlier than the late 60s. Of course, the early
chapters of Acts purport to give us some information about
early Christianity, but they are extremely sketchy and many
scholars consider them quite unreliable. Thus, even if we
think we know something about the life of Jesus, there is a
'tunnel' period between that time and the time of our first
primary sources; and it was in that tunnel period that early
Christianity seems to have undergone its most explosive and
creative developments.

Historians are an ingenious breed and they will try any means imaginable to bore holes into that tunnel. Currently much effort is being spent on reconstructing the hypothetical source Q in the hope that it may shed light on this period, but earlier this century the chief point of access into the tunnel was considered to be the pre-formed traditions embedded in the New Testament texts. This was the purpose of the project known as 'Form-Criticism', analysing the shape of the material in the Gospels or epistles to find evidence of pre-Gospel or pre-Pauline tradition. If, for instance, we could find pre-Pauline creeds, confessions, hymns or patterns of ethical instruction adopted and re-used by Paul, we might gain access to those little-known stages in Christianity during his early years as an apostle. The material might show us something of the life of the churches at that time (their worship, preaching and social patterns), and its form could be a clue to its original social context (known as its *Sitz im Leben*).

A special feature of this enquiry was the desire to chart the cultural development of early Christianity. The Jesus movement began among Aramaic-speaking Palestinian Jews, but it rapidly took hold among Greek-speaking Jews, both in Palestine and in the Diaspora, and within a remarkably short time the Christian churches were made up largely of non-Jews. How did Christianity effect these cultural transitions and what were the main cultural influences on its early theological developments? Did its thought-patterns remain primarily Jewish or were they Hellenized, and if the latter, in what respects and at what stage? These are the questions addressed by the form of enquiry known as 'History of Religions', which tries to place Christianity in its first-century religious environment and to trace its development in relation to its cultural environment.

It is easy to see how 'History of Religions' questions relate to analysis of early Christian traditions. Where do the recovered fossils of early Christian thought belong within the cultural development of early Christianity? Are they, form critics asked, from a Palestinian environment, or from a Hellenized Jewish context, or do they represent the thinking of non-Jewish Hellenistic churches? These categories have in fact proved to be far too rigid, but such questions represent an intense (and theologically loaded) interest in how, when and in what respects Christianity became 'Hellenized'.

The two texts from Colossians we will consider in this chapter are prime targets for this sort of enquiry. What do we know about the early development of Christology? How did the preacher from Nazareth come to be placed in the category of the divine, and what stages can be traced in this development? Col. 1.15-20 is clearly similar in form to some other Christological passages in the New Testament (e.g. Phil. 2.6-11; 1 Tim. 3.16) and, like them, seems to be a pre-formed tradition quoted by the author of our letter. It is particularly interesting for the full role it attributes to Christ in the creation and redemption of the whole cosmos. How, when and why did Christians come to talk of Christ *like this*? What cultural influences does this fragment of early Christology betray? Our other passage, Col. 3.18–4.1, is interesting from another perspective. It is the earliest Christian example of a 'code' of duties and reflects interest in household roles as a specific sphere of Christian morality. Is this a purely Christian invention, or does it owe something to contemporary (Jewish or Hellenistic) morality? Is it, in form and content, parallel to anything in the wider cultural environment of early Christianity, and, if so, what is suggested by its incorporation into the Christian moral tradition?

If you have read the previous chapters of this book, you will not be surprised to hear that these historical questions are connected to theological interests and agendas. The early development of Christology is obviously a sensitive matter for Christian theology, not least at the present time when Christology is under renewed scrutiny. Was this way of talking about Christ a 'natural', even a 'necessary', development from belief in the resurrection, or did it fundamentally distort the Christian faith? For some scholars, as we shall see, the 'Jewishness' of Christian beliefs is of cardinal theological importance, while others consider Hellenistic influence to have been a natural, even a welcome, development. At stake here is one's view of what sort of religion early Christianity was and what turns in its development were helpful or disastrous. In relation to the 'household code' in 3.18–4.1, the debate is influenced both by this cultural question and by feminist and liberationist theologies. Does this code represent the uncritical adoption of Hellenistic morality, or has it been mediated through Judaism and/or thoroughly Christianized in its adoption? And does it represent the injection of a hierarchical and patriarchal ethos into early Christianity, ruining its early 'egalitarian' stance? We shall keep our ears attuned to the influence of these ideological factors in scholarly debates.

The Form and Structure of the Colossian Hymn

A close reading of the first chapter of Colossians reveals that the immediacy of the address to 'you' Colossians gets lost somewhere after 1.11, returning at 1.21 after several verses describing the status and achievement of Christ. Moreover, those verses are full of predicative statements about Christ (in the form, 'he is', or 'who is'), often in some kind of balance with one another. Scholarship around the turn of the century set about closer study of these verses, comparing them with similarly 'poetic' acclamations of Christ in Phil. 2.6-11 and 1 Tim. 3.16 and with the forms of hymns to deities in Hellenistic religion. Subsequently scholars began to conclude that Col. 1.15-20 was a pre-formed Christological 'hymn', preceded by a piece of liturgical (perhaps baptismal) material in Col. 1.13-14. It is possible, of course, that the author of Colossians simply put the statements in Col. 1.15-20 together himself (some scholars still think so), but the amount of unusual vocabulary that clusters in these verses, the fact that several of their details are not immediately relevant to the context, and the parallel phenomenon of Christological 'hymns' elsewhere in the New Testament strongly support the notion that this is indeed a 'ready-made' piece of tradition.

Whether it should be called a 'hymn' is a moot point, depending on one's definition of 'hymns' (see Fowl). One might expect in a hymn some direct address to God (or Christ), which is lacking here; and this short passage in its present form does not correspond exactly to anything we find in the Psalms or in Hellenistic hymns. We know that early Christians sang 'hymns' (see Col. 3.16), though whether this passage derives from one, or was originally part of some 'confession' or even 'catechism' is uncertain. In any case, the elevated and symmetrical phraseology of this passage makes it look decidedly poetic, and we may perhaps call it 'hymnic' in a loose sense. We may not be able to say anything specific about its *Sitz im Leben* beyond its use in early Christian worship or instruction, but if we could analyse its shape, its emphases and the cultural contexts of its language about Christ, it could still tell us something about the development of Christology at a primitive stage. (How primitive depends, of course, on the dating of Colossians, which depends on its authorship; see Chapter 2. But even those who take Colossians to be deutero-Pauline date the letter not long after Paul's death, so that this pre-formed piece of Christology would have been composed no later than the 60s, and possibly much earlier.)

Given this tantalizing prospect, a huge amount of effort has been expended on analysis of this passage. The first task is to analyse the structure of the passage—a source of endless pleasure for those with tidy minds who like to 'rediscover' patterns, parallels and symmetries. The majority of scholars have concluded that the passage is shaped around the matching clauses 'who is the image' (v. 15) and 'who is the beginning' (v. 18b; the versification of our texts is a little unhelpful). The pattern of the phrases is obviously only really appreciable in the original Greek, and those who can read Greek should turn to the Greek text right away. For those who cannot read Greek I offer the following over-literal translation, which keeps as close as possible to the order and pattern of the Greek clauses. If you look at this closely enough, you will find plenty of phrases that match, balance and echo one another, and I would encourage you to mark these up yourself (on a photocopy if this is not your own book!). Scholars have tried many different ways of analysing this structure, but your own analysis is probably just as valid—and, for you, far more interesting!

Who is the image of the invisible God,
    the first-born of all creation,
  for in him were created all things
  in heaven and on earth,
  visible and invisible,

whether thrones or dominions,
whether powers or authorities,
all things were created through him and for him.

And he is before all things,
  and all things hold together in him,
And he is the head of the body, the church.

Who is the beginning,
  the first-born from the dead,
that in all things he might be pre-eminent,
for in him all the fullness was pleased to dwell,
and through him to reconcile all things to him(self),
making peace by the blood of his cross, through him,
whether things on earth or things in heaven.

The way I have set the passage out predisposes you to regard it as composed of two longish stanzas (some scholars use the Greek term, strophes), with three lines in between. You may decide, on independent analysis, that some other shape is better, but this is how the consensus of scholarship has emerged. You will notice that the two stanzas match each other very well in their beginnings but less so in subsequent lines, though there are multiple uses of the phrase 'all things' and of the prepositional phrases 'in him' and 'through him'. What is more, the content of the two stanzas seems to be roughly matched, the first covering Christ and creation, the second Christ and redemption. It is harder to see what to do with the middle lines (the first and third clearly match with the phrase 'And he is'); some have placed them with the first stanza, others regard them as an 'intermediate stanza'.

When you have studied and marked this passage up for yourself, you may be impressed by the degree of symmetry in matching words and clauses, while also noting that some parts seem to fit less well. This leads us to consider the possibility that, in its original form, the 'hymn' was more or less fully symmetrical, but that it has been edited ('redacted') by the inclusion of additional words or phrases. Certainly, the more scholars have been impressed by the symmetries they have found, the more they have been tempted to try to 'recover' a perfect original (e.g. Robinson). Some have 'recovered' something more perfect than others (finding matching numbers of syllables, or elaborate chiastic structures, or reconstructing hypothetical 'lost' lines), but a broad range of scholars have regarded two clauses as especially likely to be editorial additions to the original. The first of these is the phrase 'the church' at the end of the 'intermediate' stanza. Up to this point the 'hymn' has been about Christ and creation, and this reference to the church looks odd as an anticipation of the talk of redemption in the second stanza. Without the phrase 'the church', the 'hymn' would acclaim Christ as head of simply 'the body', which could refer to the whole cosmos (cf. 2.10); and it is rather like the author of Colossians to tack on extra genitives to other nouns (e.g. 'the word of truth, the gospel' in 1.5; cf. 1.24). The other phrase that looks like an addition is 'making peace by the blood of his cross' (the penultimate line of the second stanza). Grammatically, there are difficulties in seeing how this fits alongside 'through him', and theologically, the hymn has thus far celebrated salvation through the resurrection ('first born from the dead') not the cross, and it would be rather like Paul (or a Pauline disciple) to make sure that some reference to the cross was inserted (many think Paul did something similar in Phil. 2.8, adding to that 'hymn' the phrase 'even death on a cross').

There are other parts of the hymn that have been regarded as editorial additions, inserted either by the author of Colossians or at a stage before him, but these two have the strongest support. They offer us the prospect of recovering an original hymn and then tracing how it has been edited and its theology reshaped: in other words, we could actually watch here a *process of development* in early Christology. Nowadays there is perhaps rather less confidence in this method of 'recovery' than there was a generation ago. We may ask, for instance, if we are right to assume that the 'hymn' once ran more smoothly and symmetrically than it does now. There is also a certain weariness after decades of conflicting attempts to prove what was the 'original'; in this field at least, New Testament scholars are today rather less tolerant of attempts to 'recover' hypothetical lost sources. The current emphasis on the final form of the text, in its final context, leads to an impatience with unprovable hypotheses; we may reach the point when scholars find that, since no one knows, finally no one cares (see Morgan, p. 129). On the other hand, if literary-critical and theological factors combine in suggesting that what is before us is a secondary and edited version (as is arguably the case in the two examples noted above), it is hard to dispel altogether the suggestion of an early hymn that has undergone some changes. Recent attempts to find adequate balance in the present form of the hymn (e.g. by Wright) cannot be judged a success, so that the question at least remains open, and those who are prepared to risk hypotheses (as all historians sometimes do) will not regard this sort of enquiry as illegitimate.

Cultural and Religious Influences on the Colossian Hymn

As we noted at the beginning, the particular fascination of the Colossian hymn lies in what it represents of early Christology and how it reached this level. Can we locate this 'hymn', in its original or in its final form, in a wider cultural environment? Even a little knowledge indicates that Christians did not invent the sort of language used here, nor were they the first to apply it to some exalted or divine figure. So what were the religious and cultural influences on this formation of Christology?

Scholars have given widely divergent answers to this question, and it is initially quite baffling to find such a range of views, which are usually supported by numerous references to 'parallels'. It may be helpful to describe two alternative, though somewhat extreme, options that have played a part in the history of this debate, and then to reflect on the methods and procedures used in this activity.

We may first describe the thesis proposed by Ernst Käsemann in a famous essay of 1949 (see Further Reading for the translation). Like everything Käsemann wrote, this essay needs to be read two or three times before its full implications are grasped, but it is well worth the effort, since its combination of historical and theological analysis is extremely stimulating. Käsemann gave a pioneering analysis of the structure of the Colossian 'hymn', detecting the two editorial additions we noted above. What is more, he considered that with the removal of those two phrases, the original hymn had nothing distinctively Christian about it, and was in fact a pre-Christian Gnostic hymn. This was in line with the widespread conviction in the Bultmannian school that early Hellenistic Christianity was decisively influenced by Gnosticism, and that other early expressions of Christology (e.g. the Johannine prologue and the Philippian 'hymn') were also Christianized versions of a Gnostic redeemer myth.

Thus it is in Gnosticism that Käsemann finds the origins of the notion of an Archetypal Man who encompasses the whole cosmos, and the myth of a Redeemer who re-integrates and restores that world. This Gnostic myth, Käsemann thought, was present in the Colossian hymn 'in a form characteristic of Hellenistic Judaism' (p. 155), its influence being traceable in texts about Wisdom or the Word (*Logos*) from Philo and the Wisdom of Solomon (both from Alexandria). This Gnostic source has, however, been decisively reshaped by its intro-duction into Christianity. It now functions as a Christian confession, located in a baptismal context (Käsemann deduced this from the baptismal allusions in its introduction in vv. 13-14). The additions of the phrases 'the church' and 'making peace through the blood of the cross' have tied the cosmic mythology to a particular historical circumstance, and the association with baptism has shown that this redemption is not some timeless process, but has been made historically and existentially real in the proclamation of the forgiveness of sins. Thus Käsemann insists that the purpose of the passage as a whole is not to expand Christ's redemptive work to a cosmic scale, but to root and apply this otherwise mytho-logical language in the proclamation of the church, which is the concrete manifestation of the new creation celebrated in the hymn.

A quite different interpretation of the religious context of the hymn was offered somewhat speculatively by C.F. Burney, and subsequently expanded by some scholars, recently by N.T. Wright. Burney suggested that all the state-ments about Christ in this passage arose from 'an elaborate exposition of the first word in Genesis', *bereshith* ('in the beginning'), which had been connected with the famous passage about wisdom in Prov. 8.22. Most of Burney's work is a philological analysis of the meaning of this verse in

Proverbs, but at the end of his article he suggested that the reference in Colossians to Christ as the 'firstborn of creation' was a direct echo of that verse, and its connection with Gen. 1.1 led to further statements about the 'beginning' status of Christ. Indeed, since the Hebrew word *bereshith* can have a variety of senses ('in the beginning', 'by the beginning') and the word *reshith* can mean 'beginning', 'head' and 'sum-total', Burney thought that all of the statements about Christ in the Colossian hymn arose simply from Paul's own reflection on the range of senses possible in these two Old Testament texts.

This suggestion has greatly appealed to those who see early Christology as a wholly inner-Jewish phenomenon. N.T. Wright, for instance, places Burney's theory within the framework of 'mainstream Judaism', specifically its monotheism and its celebration of God's dual work in creation and redemption. Wright considers that the reference to 'the image of the invisible God' echoes what is said of humanity in Gen. 1.26, which suggests that the role of humanity (or Israel, its representative) has been focused onto Christ, who, like Wisdom, represents God's role as Creator and Redeemer. Thus Christ is here viewed not in terms of a Gnostic Redeemer, but in the wholly Jewish terms appropriate to God, creating an anomalous, but theologically fruitful, 'christological monotheism' (p. 114).

Readers may themselves assess the strengths and weaknesses of these two opposing explanations of the Colossian hymn, or of others that take a more mediating position. They represent, in fact, two contrasting fashions in cultural and theological analysis of early Christianity. Käsemann's solution comes from an era when German scholarship was convinced of the presence and influence of a fully developed pre-Christian Gnosticism, complete with its own redeemer myth. Since the 1950s that thesis has fallen on hard times, not least because the sources on which it depended do not prove the existence of a pre-Christian Gnostic Redeemer figure. In fact, Käsemann himself soon abandoned talk of Gnostic cosmic forces and interpreted early Christianity more in relation to Jewish apocalyptic theology. On the other hand, Gnosticism itself is now viewed as heavily influenced

by Judaism at its origins. Even if there was no pre-Christian
Gnostic redeemer myth, there may have been Jewish-Gnostic
speculations about creation and the role of the Man/Word/
Image in shaping that creation—speculations that arguably
stand close to the sort of claims made for Christ in this hymn
(see Fossum).

Wright's approach, on the other hand, is symptomatic of a
post-War move to interpret early Christianity as primarily a
Jewish phenomenon, a move influenced by a reaction against
anti-Semitism and by the discovery of the Dead Sea Scrolls.
One highly influential figure in this change was the
Tübingen scholar, Martin Hengel, who regarded the high
expressions of Christology as a very early development
explicable in wholly Jewish terms. In attributing to Christ a
role in creation, Christians were only concluding that God's
eschatological agent must have had his pre-eminent role
from the very beginning, a move paralleled in Jewish
thinking about wisdom and the law. 'This step was not a
gnostic, syncretistic falsification but a necessary last conse-
quence of primitive Christian thinking. Here the community
moved, and could not do otherwise: from a historical and
theological perspective it was quite right to do so' (Hengel,
p. 95). It is not difficult to detect the theological preferences
that lie behind this loaded statement and behind many
contemporary attempts to depict Christian beginnings as an
inner-Jewish phenomenon, untainted by 'pagan' thoughts or
practices.

To discern the theological motives behind particular historical reconstructions is not to discredit them; in fact, it is
precisely the combination of historical and theological interests that makes the analysis of the Colossian hymn so interesting. Perhaps loaded terms like 'syncretistic' are best
avoided—or else enthusiastically embraced, since every religion, including Judaism and Christianity, has flourished only
through creative engagement with its contemporary cultural
and religious context. In fact, in the case of the Colossian
Christology, the most impressive parallels are probably to be
found in reflection about mediator figures current in
Hellenistic Judaism, which was 'Hellenistic' precisely in its
selective use and adaptation of Hellenism. Käsemann's

notion of a pre-Christian Gnostic hymn has long been abandoned (the positive interest in creation and resurrection seems incompatible with Gnosticism), and Burney's thesis draws far too much out of a single Hebrew term. Nowadays, almost all analyses of the Colossian hymn agree that some of the closest analogies to its Christological statements are to be found in some passages in Philo and in the Wisdom of Solomon. Philo, for instance, has a developed theology of the *Logos* (word, reason, speech), whom he describes as God's agent in creation and sometimes equates with Wisdom (the mother of all things) and with the Image of God (the prototype of creation). In the Wisdom of Solomon, the depiction of Wisdom in Proverbs 8 (cf. Sir. 1 and 24) is considerably expanded under Hellenistic influence, and Wisdom is described as an entity which 'fashioned all things'; she 'pervades and penetrates all things' and is 'a pure emanation of the glory of the Almighty' (7.21–8.1; the whole passage should be read; see further Dunn, pp. 163-212).

To cite these as 'parallels' is not to suggest that they are the source of the Colossian hymn (scholars sometimes confuse these two notions), but that they are close analogies that indicate that it was possible for Jews, influenced by Hellenism, to develop speculation about figures who co-created the universe alongside God. Presumably this was equally possible for Christian Jews, whose high evaluation of Jesus as 'Lord' would make it easy to attach to him such notions. To suggest that there was a ready-made 'Wisdom theology' into which Jesus could be neatly slotted, is oversimplistic. Rather, what we have is a creative theological development in which Christians, like Hellenized Jews, merged Hellenistic theological and philosophical notions about God and the world with Jewish texts concerning Wisdom and the creative Speech or Image of God, and crystallized both in a distinctive Christian manner in relation to the risen Christ. In the next chapter we will reflect further on the effects of this extremely significant development. For now, I hope merely to have shown that the scholarly effort to analyse the form of this 'hymn' and to detect the cultural influences upon it is not some abstruse exercise. It is a limited but necessary part of uncovering both what this text means and what it indicates of the early development of Christology, which is, after all, the heart of the Christian faith.

The Household Code

The other passage in Colossians that looks most like a preformed tradition is the set of exhortations contained in 3.18–4.1. This passage is clearly a unit with six matching instructions, in three pairs: wives and husbands, children and fathers, slaves and masters. Both in style and in content this passage seems like an island in its present context, not obviously connected to what goes before or what comes after; in fact, if you took it away, you could move easily from 3.17 to 4.2 without realizing anything was missing in between. What is more, there are striking similarities between this passage and some others in early Christian literature. In the New Testament the obvious parallels are Eph. 5.21–6.9 and 1 Pet. 2.18–3.7, both of which also focus on relationships in the household. There are also passages that invoke a similar attitude of 'submission' in relation to Christians' station in life, in relation to the state authorities (Rom. 13.1-7; 1 Pet. 2.13-17; Tit. 3.1-2), in address to slaves (1 Tim. 6.1-2), in male–female relationships (1 Tim. 2.8-15) and concerning general relationships in the Christian community (e.g. Tit. 2.1-10; 1 Pet. 5.1-5). Many of these types of instruction can be found, though rather less clearly organized, in subsequent early Christian literature, as for instance in *Didache* 4.9-11, *Barnabas* 19.7, *1 Clement* 1.3 and 21.6-8, Polycarp, *Philippians* chs. 4–6 and Ignatius, *Polycarp* chs. 4–6.

Putting these passages together, they appear to represent a tendency to form a code of Christian duties, generally known as a 'household code' (German: *Haustafel*, plural *Haustafeln*). Because of the close similarity between the passages in Colossians, Ephesians and 1 Peter, it has been tempting to try to reconstruct an original text, a written code from which all or most of these early Christian texts derive. In fact there are special factors creating the similarities between these three particular texts, the Ephesian code being derived directly from the text of Colossians and 1 Peter perhaps depending on oral or literary familiarity with the

Pauline tradition. There was probably no one 'prototype' code, but rather a common tendency in these early Christian circles to list duties relating to everyday life. It is slightly misleading to call all these codes 'household codes', since many range well beyond that context into political or ecclesial relationships. But what they do have in common is a focus on everyday responsibilities, with a strong emphasis on 'submission' or 'obedience'. And since the first example of such a code is found in Colossians, where it also has a particularly neat structure, this text has formed the focus for much debate about the origins of such codes and the implications of their adoption in early Christianity.

The discussion of the origins of Christian household codes has been under way since the beginning of this century. Although some scholars have maintained that they represent an original Christian creation, most have been impressed by the 'parallels' that have been found, notably in Stoic lists of duties, in texts on household duties found in Hellenistic Judaism (Josephus, Philo and Pseudo-Phocylides) and in a widespread philosophical debate on the proper management of the household (useful surveys of scholarship may be found in Crouch and in Balch, 'Household Codes'). One problem bedevilling this debate has been a lack of clarity concerning what sort of 'parallel' is being sought. In some cases the focus has been purely on the *topic* of the codes, but in others parallels have been sought and claimed in relation to both *topic* and *form*. In a general sense (and in some items of vocabulary) the codes bear some resemblance to the lists of duties (to gods, country, parents, wife, children and friends) which we find in a range of Stoic sources, especially if we include here the early Christian codes that range beyond household matters. However, the more narrowly focused household codes are closer in theme to the philosophical debates about household management, which from Aristotle onwards tended to focus on the same three relationships as we find in the Colossian code: husbands and wives, fathers and children, masters and slaves. Since the discussion of this topic usually concerns the management of the household, the dominant ethos is typically that of control by the head of the household, an ethos that clearly matches the Christian instructions to subordinate parties to 'submit'. Thus we might say that the topic of the Colossian code and its ethos are most closely parallel to treatments of this theme by Greek and Roman popular philosophers. But what about the *form* of the code? In the Colossian (and Ephesian) code, each party is addressed directly and their reciprocal relationships are highlighted (what wives owe to husbands, what husbands owe to wives etc.). It is hard to find close parallels to this direct address and such reciprocity in the Stoic discussions of duties or in the wider debates on household management, and some have claimed that these formal features are more closely paralleled in the Jewish sources mentioned above. If the truth be told, there is no *precise* analogy to the form and theme of the Colossian code, although one can point to many sources that discuss the theme of household relationships and a few texts (both Jewish and non-Jewish) in which such relationships are viewed from both sides. The search for the nearest precise analogy has led to exaggerated claims that the Colossian code really derives from a Hellenistic-Jewish or a popular philosophical source. It would be safer to say that the Colossian code has no exact formal antecedent (i.e. it is not copied wholesale from some pre-Christian source), but that its theme and ethos are very closely related to common assumptions in the first-century world concerning the proper behaviour of members of a household. If we find the same three pairings mentioned elsewhere as in Colossians, that is hardly surprising: this is the most natural way of analysing household relationships in antiquity (slaves being an integral part of the household).

In fact, it is the very ordinariness of the assumptions of these codes that has attracted most theological attention. Did the early Christians simply adopt the *mores* of their contemporary society in these matters? Or have the codes been given a significantly different Christian ethos? Christian unease with the first alternative has been obvious ever since the growing post-Enlightenment conviction that slavery is incompatible with the ethos of the gospel; it has been notably compounded in recent years by the rise of Christian feminism which naturally baulks at the instruction here given to wives. Martin Dibelius, the form-critic who first analysed the origin of the household code, suggested that the Colossian material had been taken over largely unaltered from Stoicism (with or without the mediation of Hellenistic Judaism): the addition of the phrases 'in the Lord' or 'to the Lord' provided a superficial Christianization for fundamentally Stoic notions of what was 'fitting' (e.g. Col. 3.18). Since his day a number of attempts have been made to find a more profound Christian influence here. The phrase 'in the Lord' might be argued to provide a real change to the quality and conditions of the relationships here described (so Moule), but in fact it seems to give only a Christian motivation for behaviour that matches traditional expectations of household relations. A number of scholars have argued that the direct address to the subordinate members of each pairing (wives, children, slaves) and the reciprocal nature of the instructions indicates a special (Jewish) concern for the weaker members of society (Schweizer) or a 'balancing' of relationships in which both sides have rights as well as duties (e.g. Wright). The direct address to the subordinate members may indicate that they are given greater attention than in the traditional instructions to the *paterfamilias* (head of the household) alone. However, when one looks at the content of what the lower orders are instructed to do, it is difficult to find much evidence of 'balancing'; 'reciprocity' is present here only in that each relationship is recognized as double-sided, not in granting to the submissive partners any special rights. Simply to give instructions to slaves was not to accord them any particular 'ethical responsibility'; masters continually barked orders at them without any such fine sensibility! Moreover, is there anything specifically new or Christian in the instruction that husbands love their wives or that masters treat their slaves reasonably? Most people in the ancient world recognized that dictatorial households tended to be unhappy.

Thus apologetic attempts to find some special Christian character in this code are largely unconvincing. It is better to recognize that, for better or worse, the code represents a Christianization of traditional rulings on household relationships. One may then ask how such a phenomenon has come about. To an extent it needs no special explanation, since the early Christians were hardly able or willing to create a moral code *de novo*, and much else in early Christian ethics is also unremarkable by contemporary standards. However, a number of special explanations have been offered by scholars, for instance, that the code is meant to counter a revolutionary spirit among Hellenistic Christians, especially women and slaves (Crouch), or that it was necessary as an (indirect) apologetic move to counteract suspicions that the new Christian cult was socially radical (Balch). Such explanations would certainly make sense of the special emphasis in these codes on submission and obedience (in each case the subordinate partners are addressed first in these terms), though they hardly fit the instructions to children. In part, the code may simply represent the need for early Christianity to come to terms with the daily realities of its continued existence in the world, for which the household and the continuities of family life were to be of crucial importance. Whether one interprets this theologically as arising from the waning of hope for an immediate parousia (Dibelius), or sociologically in terms of 'community-stabilization' (MacDonald), it amounts to a crucial process of social adjustment for the early Christian movement.

Such an adjustment has been represented as a positive step, an example of 'good worldliness' (Schweizer). More recently, it has come under severe theological criticism as a lapse into hierarchical patterns of patriarchal domination which are out of step with the gospel and the earliest forms of Christian community. Thus Munro has argued that all the hierarchical passages in the Pauline letters and Colossians/ Ephesians are an interpolated overlay from a later period when patriarchal patterns became the norm. More subtly, Schüssler Fiorenza has offered a feminist reconstruction of early Christian history in which the earliest 'discipleship of equals' (represented by the baptismal slogan of Gal. 3.28) was treated ambiguously by Paul (e.g. 1 Cor. 11.2-16 and 14.33-36) and finally gave way to an ideology of patriarchalism, in which inequality and exploitation was accepted into the Christian community. It is important for this reconstruction that the household code is a 'later Christian adaptation' of Graeco-Roman or Hellenistic Jewish codes and not 'genuinely Christian' (Schüssler Fiorenza, p. 254); but this simply makes clear how much discussion of our topic is influenced by prior theological and moral definitions of 'genuine' Christianity.

However we evaluate the use of this code in Colossians, the subsequent tradition of 'duty codes' in early Christian literature indicates that our passage constitutes a watershed in early Christian ethics, the beginning of a diverse and expanding tradition in which the Christian faith became embedded in social structures, and submission or 'order' become cardinal virtues (see Horrell). In a parallel way, the inclusion of the Colossian hymn proved to be a watershed for the development of Christian theology, portraying Christ and the church on a cosmic stage and in a framework of universal reconciliation. In fact, these theological and ethical developments are not unrelated to one another, and it is the task of our next chapter to place the texts we have studied here back into the context of the letter as a whole, to sketch out its composite theology and to consider its significance in the development of early Christianity.

Further Reading

All the commentaries provide some discussion of the form and cultural background of 1.15-20 (see especially those by Lohse, Martin, O'Brien and Schweizer); most recent commentaries do the same in introducing 3.18–4.1. See also:

Balch, D.L., *Let Wives Be Submissive* (Chico: Scholars Press, 1981). On household codes.

—'Household Codes', in D.E. Aune (ed.), *Greco-Roman Literature and the New Testament* (Atlanta: Scholars Press, 1988), pp. 25-50.

Burney, C.F., 'Christ as the APXH of Creation', *JTS* 27 (1926), pp. 160-77.

Cannon, G.E., *The Use of Traditional Materials in Colossians* (Macon, GA: Mercer University Press, 1983).

Crouch, J.E., *The Origin and Intention of the Colossian Haustafel* (Göttingen: Vandenhoeck & Ruprecht, 1972).

Dunn, J.D.G., *Christology in the Making* (London: SCM Press, 1980), pp. 163-212.

Fossum, J., 'Colossians 1.15-18a in the Light of Jewish Mysticism and Gnosticism', *NTS* 35 (1989), pp. 183-201.

Fowl, S.E., *The Story of Christ in the Ethics of Paul: An Analysis of the Function of the Hymnic Material in the Pauline Corpus* (JSNTSup, 36; Sheffield: JSOT Press, 1990).

Hartman, L., 'Some Unorthodox Thoughts on the "Household Code Form" ',
    in J. Neusner *et al.* (eds.), *The Social World of Formative Christianity
    and Judaism* (Philadelphia: Fortress Press, 1988), pp. 219-32.
Hengel, M., 'Hymns and Christology', in *Between Jesus and Paul: Studies in
    the Earliest History of Christianity* (London: SCM Press, 1983), pp. 78-
    96.
Horrell, D.G., *The Social Ethos of the Corinthian Correspondence: Interests
    and Ideology from 1 Corinthians to 1 Clement* (Edinburgh: T. & T.
    Clark, 1996).
Käsemann, E., 'A Primitive Christian Baptismal Liturgy', in *Essays on New
    Testament Themes* (London: SCM Press, 1964, pp. 149-68).
MacDonald, M.Y., *The Pauline Churches: A Socio-Historical Study of
    Institutionalization in the Pauline and Deutero-Pauline Writings*
    (Cambridge: Cambridge University Press, 1988).
Morgan, R., with J. Barton, *Biblical Interpretation* (Oxford: Oxford
    University Press, 1988), pp. 93-132.
Munro, W., *Authority in Paul and Peter: The Identification of a Pastoral
    Stratum in the Pauline Corpus and 1 Peter* (Cambridge: Cambridge
    University Press, 1983).
Robinson, J.M., 'A Formal Analysis of Colossians 1.15-20', *JBL* 76 (1957),
    pp. 270-87.
Sanders, J.T., *The New Testament Christological Hymns: Their Religious
    Background* (Cambridge: Cambridge University Press, 1971).
Schüssler Fiorenza, E., *In Memory of Her: A Feminist Theological
    Reconstruction of Christian Origins* (London: SCM Press, 1983).
    Relevant to household codes.
Schweizer, E., 'The Church as the Missionary Body of Christ', *NTS* 8
    (1961–62), pp. 1-11. Esp. pp. 6-11 on the Colossian hymn.
—'Traditional Ethical Patterns in the Pauline and Post-Pauline Letters and
    their Development (Lists of Vices and House-Tables)', in E. Best and R.
    McL. Wilson (eds.), *Text and Interpretation* (Cambridge: Cambridge
    University Press, 1979), pp. 195-210.
Wright, N.T., 'Poetry and Theology in Colossians 1.15-20', *NTS* 6 (1990), pp.
    444-68; repr. in *The Climax of the Covenant* (Edinburgh: T. & T. Clark,
    1991), pp. 99-119.

5

THE THEOLOGY OF COLOSSIANS

The Dearth of Theological Analysis

In this chapter we turn to analyse the theology of Colossians, that is, the way it speaks about God, Christ, the universe and humanity, enquiring whether our letter offers a unified theological vision. It is remarkable how rarely New Testament scholars engage in a direct theological analysis of the whole letter, although it is heavily theological in content. It will be helpful first to suggest some of the reasons for this dearth of theological analysis; that will also serve to clarify the particular stance I have chosen to adopt here.

In the first place, a large percentage of the analysis of Colossians has taken place in the form of commentaries on the letter, and the writing of commentaries encourages a piecemeal approach in which detailed questions of exegesis inhibit a broad perspective on the letter as a whole. Moreover, the predominant historical-critical modes of exegesis place the greatest emphasis on linguistic and historical matters, such as the sources of the thought of Colossians or its parallels in the religious environment of the first century. What the text actually says is drowned out by reference to who else in antiquity said something similar.

Secondly, the increasing consensus that the letter is pseudonymous has implicitly downgraded its theological value. When Colossians is dubbed 'deutero-Pauline' that label typically signifies an assessment that the letter is secondary not only in chronology but also in significance. Thus, the tendency of scholars to emphasize contrasts between

Colossians and the 'assured' Pauline letters nearly always directs attention away from Colossians to earlier, more pristine documents, which are generally treated as of greater theological weight. Correspondingly, discussions of 'Pauline theology' (a common theme) typically leave Colossians out of account.

Thirdly, the task of reconstructing the target of Colossians has proved so absorbing that scholars tend to treat the letter simply as a response, and thus to analyse its theology only with respect to its polemical functions. As I noted above (p. 38), our comprehension of the force of the letter would indeed be aided by a clear delineation of the problems to which it responds. Yet the nature of the evidence has forced us to adopt rather sceptical conclusions about our ability to reconstruct the target of the letter (Chapter 3), so that to analyse its theology primarily from this 'response' perspective would render our analysis extremely insecure. What is more, it is not clear that the letter is to be regarded as *wholly* absorbed by the counter-ideology; the 'direction' of its thought should not be reduced to its possible contextual motives. In other words, the theology of the letter must be taken seriously for what it says, not simply for why it might be saying it.

Finally, full engagement with the theology of the letter has often been inhibited by the reductionism that finds interest only in how the author used and adapted pre-formed materials. As we have seen (Chapter 4), the attempt to trace pre-formed material is neither illegitimate nor unfruitful, but if it becomes all-absorbing it distracts attention away from the full body of the text to the putative additions, subtractions or realignments that the author has performed with his source material. Such modifications may indeed indicate something of the special tendencies of Colossians, but we should still take with full seriousness the whole body of the text, including what the author has adopted but left unchanged. In study of the gospels, the emphasis has recently and helpfully shifted from 'redaction criticism', which sometimes became narrowly concerned with the evangelists' alteration of their sources, to a holistic analysis of the complete text in its final form. If the same shift were to occur here, the whole of Colossians could be analysed as a unit, without excessive concentration on the author's putative changes to his sources. As we shall see, this is particularly important in the evaluation of the Colossian 'hymn' (1.15-20), whose original cosmic scope has arguably been supplemented by the author of the letter, but not obliterated.

In what follows I hope to orientate readers of Colossians to its interlocking theological themes, taking into consideration the whole text and declining to pay prime attention either to its possible functions in counteracting the 'philosophy' or to its employment of pre-formed materials. Since an *analysis* of the text must go beyond mere *repetition* of its statements, I will here engage with the text in a spirit of critical sympathy, trying to take seriously the goals and theological achievements of the letter while recognizing it as a historical product from which we stand, inevitably, at some conceptual distance. My concluding remarks will indicate in outline some aspects of the dialogue that may be opened up between Colossians and contemporary Christian theology.

Theology for a Burgeoning International Religion

The letter to the Colossians represents a crucial stage in the development of Pauline theology. (In the light of Chapter 2, the adjective 'Pauline' is here left deliberately ambiguous.) We find here an important and influential attempt to provide an integrated view of reality which makes its starting-point and touchstone the key distinctive of the early church, its faith in Christ. Spurred, in part, by the 'philosophy' it targets and inspired by earlier formulations of Christian faith (e.g. the 'hymn'), our author offers a comprehensive vision of truth—cosmic and human, spiritual and material, divine and mundane—whose focal point is Christology. The theology of Colossians is at every point Christological, and it is the success of the author in disclosing Christ as the centre of all reality that integrates and energizes the letter.

Such a comprehensive Christology fits perfectly the stage in Christian development to which this letter belongs. In the Pauline sphere, at least, it was clear already in the 50s of the first century that the church was a sociological novelty which could fit neither within the Jewish community nor among the multifarious cults of Graeco-Roman religion (see e.g. 1 Cor. 10.32). While including, of course, both Jews and Gentiles, the Pauline churches began to see themselves as social entities which transcended previous ethnic grouping; they were new communities which relativized the social, ethnic and gender distinctions dominant in the Graeco-Roman world, while also belonging to one another in some higher sense as 'the church of God' (see e.g. Gal. 1.13; 3.28). In terms of its beliefs, what set 'the church' apart from both Jews and non-Jews was its understanding of God *in terms of Christ* (1 Cor. 1.22-25): its unity and its life were understood to derive from its existence 'in Christ', and it constituted corporately 'the body of Christ'. Thus, the more apparent the church's social uniqueness, the more it would become conscious of its distinguishing and unifying basis in Christology.

Colossians represents this stage of heightened Christological self-consciousness that is also sufficiently confident to claim that the church's 'secret' is the secret of the universe. The letter opens with the assertion that the gospel, 'the message of truth', has been 'bearing fruit and growing in the whole world' (1.5-6), and it later reinforces this sense of universal spread with the claim that the gospel has been preached 'to every creature under heaven' (1.23). The apostle's task is to 'warn everyone and teach everyone in all wisdom, so as to present everyone perfect in Christ' (1.28), a sentence notable for its repeated universalisms. The theology of the letter thus reflects a sense that the church's universal conquest is, if not yet complete, nonetheless well under way (cf. the reference to [numerical?] growth in 2.19). Thus, no nation, no human being, indeed no 'creature' is beyond the reach of the gospel, whose truth must embrace them all and bring them to 'perfection' in Christ. This universal claim is dramatically repeated in a significant rewording of an old baptismal formula (3.11). If one compares this verse with its precursors in Gal. 3.28 and 1 Cor. 12.13, it is clear that the embrace of the formula is more self-consciously international, now including 'barbarian' and 'Scythian', that is, the least 'civilized' representatives of humanity. But the conclusion of the verse also indicates the corresponding expansive thrust of early Christian theology. It is not merely that all these classes of people are 'one in Christ Jesus' (Gal. 3.28), or that they have been baptized into one body, the body of Christ (1 Cor. 12.12-13): rather, Col. 3.11 makes the far broader claim that 'Christ is all and in all' (*ta panta kai en pasin Christos*). Hence a formula which originally claimed the reunification and remaking of humankind in baptism here reflects the expansion of Christian horizons and celebrates the meaning of Christ in the most universal terms possible (see also Meeks). As we shall see, that term 'all things' (*ta panta*) reverberates throughout Colossians, connecting all life and truth to Christ.

Colossians is thus sufficiently bold to proclaim Christ as the key to the universe, or, to use its favourite metaphor, as the 'mystery' (or 'secret') of all reality. Christ constitutes quite simply 'the mystery of God' (2.2) and it is in him that may be found hidden 'all the treasures of wisdom and knowledge' (2.3). To preach the gospel is to preach 'the mystery which is Christ' (4.3), that is, 'the mystery which has been hidden throughout the ages and generations but has now been revealed to his saints' (1.26-27). Thus the deepest reality (God), the eternal secrets (of the ages) and the profoundest truths (of wisdom) are all unlocked by Christ. It is perhaps no accident that our author describes Christ as 'mystery', since this term represented the supreme commodity offered both by Jewish apocalyptic theology and by Graeco-Roman 'mystery' cults. Correspondingly, the benefit of faith is repeatedly described as 'knowledge' (1.6, 9, 10, 27; 2.2, 3; 3.10), 'wisdom' (1.9, 28; 2.3, 23; 3.16; 4.5) and 'understanding' (1.9; 2.2), terms of international currency in both Jewish and Gentile traditions. Here a burgeoning international religion claims access to 'all the treasures of wisdom and knowledge'; they are to be found in its distinctive cult focus and saviour, Christ.

Christ as the Core of Reality

The central significance of Christ in Colossians means that every aspect of its theology may be viewed in terms of its relationship to Christology. The thorough integration of its theology makes it difficult to dissect neatly, but we may note these eight interconnected features:

1. *Christ and Creation*. The most striking feature of the 'hymn' in 1.15-20 is the role it accords to Christ in the creation of the universe. To describe him as 'first-born of all creation' (1.15) might signify merely some precedence or priority over the rest of creation: 'first-born' could connote temporal priority or (metaphorically) superiority of status, but the genitive 'of all creation' leaves initially ambiguous whether Christ is to be counted among the creation or over it. However, the following verse (1.16) indicates that Christ is in a quite different category from creation, since all things (*ta panta*) are said to have been created 'in him', 'through him' and 'for him'. The scope of the items mentioned in this verse indicates that this creation is not some partial or local event but the sum total of physical and 'spiritual' reality. Christ is not said here to be their creator: they are created (by God) 'in him'; but neither is his role simply that of agent or mediator, since the 'in him' and 'through him' are supplemented by the striking 'for him' (*eis auton*) at the end of 1.16. Comparing this formula with that in 1 Cor. 8.6 (another confessional statement) highlights the importance of this addition, since there 'all things' are said to come into existence 'from' and 'to' (*eis*) God, while Christ is only the agent 'through whom' they exist. Thus here in Colossians Christ is seen not merely as the instrument of creation, the tool of God's creative power, but as the one to whom all creation tends, the goal and purpose of its existence.

This integration of Christ into the very rationale of creation is strengthened by the reference in 1.17 to the coherence of 'all things' in Christ: 'all things hold together in him'. What is claimed here is thus not merely some primaeval role in bringing creation about, nor some 'headship' imposed from without on an alien world, but an inner relation between Christ and creation concerning its meaning and integrity. To be sure, much here is expressed in suggestive but ill-defined terms, through multivalent prepositions like 'in', 'through' and 'to'. Yet the scope of the claim could hardly have been greater. Whatever the origin of such phraseology (see

Chapter 4), the key to creation is here found not in 'Wisdom', 'Logos' or hypostatized 'Man', but in the One whom Christians know and worship as Christ.

It is important to observe how the claims of the first 'strophe' of the 'hymn' (1.15-17) match those to be found in the second strophe. This celebrates Christ as *archē* (beginning, authority) in relation to the resurrection—'the first-born from the dead, that he might be pre-eminent in all things (*en pasin*)' (1.18). As the founding event of the new creation, the resurrection establishes Christ as supreme, although the description of this as a newly attained status, and the subsequent reference to the reconciliation of all things (1.20), creates some tension between the first and second strophes. It may be that, historically, the celebration of Christ as the Resurrected Lord (cf. Phil. 2.9-11) and the declaration of a renewal of creation in baptism (Col. 3.11) were the prior Christian convictions that led only later to the sorts of claims we have found in the first strophe. But our concern here is not with the stages of development *behind* Colossians, but with what confronts us in its text. And there Christ is seen as the agent, meaning and ruler of creation from first to last.

2. *Christ and God*. This role of Christ in creation inevitably brings Christ into the closest possible association with God. As we have noted, Christ is described in Colossians as 'the mystery of God' (2.2), and although he is never described *as* God (*theos*), it is clear that our author could not reflect on God without reflecting also on Christ. Where Christ is described as 'the image of the invisible God' (1.15), the phrase suggests making God's presence visible and God's power effective, since 'images' in antiquity not only reveal but also channel the effectiveness of their 'prototype'. Something like this may be reflected in the mysterious comment that 'all the fullness was pleased to dwell in him' (1.19; commentators dispute what is the subject of this clause). That phrase may be given some explanation in 2.9 where it is said that 'all the fullness of deity (*theotēs*) dwells in him bodily/substantially (*sōmatikōs*)': that gets about as near to calling Christ 'God' as it is possible to go without actually doing so.

Certainly in terms of function, what is said of Christ in this letter is what is attributed elsewhere to God, for instance, that creation is 'for him' and that he is 'all and in all' (1.16; 3.11; cf. Rom. 11.36; 1 Cor. 8.6; 15.28). Within this letter, reference can be made to 'the kingdom of God' (4.11) and 'the kingdom of his beloved Son' (1.13) without any apparent distinction between the two. The subordination of Christ to God characteristic of some of Paul's statements (e.g. 1 Cor. 3.23; 11.3; 15.27-28) is here dispelled under the impact of the global Christological claims. Colossians thus contains some of the 'highest' Christology in the New Testament (comparable to Revelation) without attempting to define in ontological terms the relationship between Christ and God it portrays. Indeed, with hindsight it seems almost mischievously to invite the Christological battles of later centuries!

3. *Christ and Salvation*. Taken on their own, there is nothing in 1.15-17 that would prepare one to expect that there was any need of salvation, either for humanity or for the cosmos. Yet these statements are here part of a wider Christian discourse, in which Christ is hailed as saviour, and in which believers know themselves to be rescued from the power of darkness and transferred into the kingdom of God's Son (1.13-14). This redemptive reality is indeed celebrated in the second strophe of the 'hymn' (1.18b-20), which begins by alluding to the resurrection ('first-born from the dead'), affirms the reconciliation of all things to Christ (1.20) and includes near its end a reference to 'the blood of the cross' (1.20). Thus the hymn itself contains a tension between two senses in which Christ is 'all in all'. On the one hand, he is such as the one through whom and for whom (*eis auton*) all things were created; but on the other, he is pre-eminent because of the resurrection and because all things have been reconciled to him (*eis auton*). The first seems a universal claim, timeless, or at least from the beginning of time; the second is connected to an event (the resurrection) and presupposes that the creaturely relation of 'all things' to Christ had somehow gone astray and needed to be restored. This is the first of several (parallel) tensions we will find in the theology of Colossians, and it is important at this stage neither to deny nor to dilute it, but simply to note it as part

of a complex picture. The theology of Colossians unequivo-
cally posits an act of salvation; but that act is put against a
wider horizon where all things already find their meaning in
Christ.

For the moment we may leave this paradox aside and deal
instead with a smaller and partly illusory one. As we saw in
Chapter 4, many scholars think that the phrase 'making
peace by the blood of his cross' (1.20) was an addition by our
author to the earlier 'hymn', linking the salvation-event to
the cross, rather than to the resurrection. It is certainly the
case that the subsequent application of the 'hymn' to the
addressees (1.21-23) makes special reference to Christ's
death and not to the resurrection, and that 2.14-15 further
expounds the meaning of the crucifixion. Yet it hardly makes
sense to play off one against the other. In Col. 2.11-13 (as in
earlier Pauline letters) the cross and the resurrection fit
closely together in the scheme of salvation, and if 2.14-15
focuses specifically on the cross, 3.1-4 comments on the
significance of the resurrection. A closer look at these latter
two passages will reveal important aspects of the soteriology
of the letter.

In 2.14-15 salvation is described under the twin aspects of
forgiveness of sins and defeat of the 'powers'. The forgiveness
of sins is a special emphasis in this letter (cf. 1.14; 3.13) and
it is here dramatically portrayed through a gloriously mixed
metaphor concerning a record of debt. In 2.14 the unusual
term *cheirographon* is used, normally translated 'bond' or
'record': it seems to mean an IOU recording debts or obligations. This is a vivid metaphor for the sins that condemn
humankind and it is described here as dealt with by (a) eras-
ing it, (b) setting it aside, and (c) nailing it to the cross. One
should not attempt to combine these three into a single
image; they are just different ways of describing the over-
ruling of a debt-bond, the last clearly related to the crucifixion but otherwise somewhat obscure. The focus then shifts
in 2.15 to the treatment of the 'powers and authorities' (see
section 4). The precise image is unfortunately not clear, since
the key verb in 2.15 could mean either (a) that God 'disarmed' the powers, or (b) that Christ 'divested himself' of
them, or (c) that he simply 'stripped off' (cf. 2.11), and made a

public example of the powers. In favour of the first option is that God has been the subject from 2.13 and 'disarming' would go well with the final image of disgracing the powers and displaying them as vanquished enemies in a triumphal procession. In favour of the second or third is that the verb matches that used in 2.11 and 3.9, where 'stripping off' is clearly the sense; perhaps by his death Christ 'strips off' the body and/or 'sloughs off' the rule of the powers who control the sphere of the flesh (cf. Rom. 8.3; 2 Cor. 5.21). On any interpretation, the sense of the crucifixion as enacting (or displaying) a cosmic victory over the 'powers' is a powerful metaphor which was to spawn a long tradition of theological reflection on the cross ('Christus Victor').

In 3.1-4 and in 2.11-13 the emphasis rests on the inclusion of the believer in the death–resurrection event, with notable statements that Christians have been raised with Christ (contrast Rom. 6.1-8). Thus the life of the believer is dependent on and totally bound up with the life of the risen Christ ('Christ who is your life', 3.4), and such a 'realized eschatology' places the emphasis on the 'things above' rather than fostering a hope of unfulfilled 'things to come'. We shall explore these features further below (section 7).

4. *Christ and the Powers.* The references to the powers in Colossians confront us with a number of theological tensions parallel to that I noted above (pp. 82-83). In the first part of the 'hymn', the creation made in and for Christ includes 'things in heaven and things on earth, things visible and invisible, whether thrones or dominions or rulers (*archai*) or powers (*exousiai*)' (1.16). These entities seem to fit in the category of what is 'in heaven' and 'invisible', referring, that is, to spiritual realities deeper than human power structures. Yet the second part of the 'hymn', as I noted, seems to presuppose some disintegration or rebellion in the creation, in that all things need to be reconciled to Christ, including 'things on earth and things in heaven' (1.20). If the 'things in heaven' include the 'thrones' etc., they are portrayed as having somehow fallen out of unity, or out of friendship, with Christ.

The language of 1.20 strongly suggests a reintegration of the creation. The 'things in heaven' are 'reconciled to Christ' apparently in the sense that they come back into unity with him; there is a 'making of peace' through the blood of the cross. Yet, as we have just seen, when the cross is mentioned in relation to the 'rulers (*archai*) and powers (*exousiai*)' in 2.15, it is depicted as an event in which they are disarmed, or at least publicly disgraced and led in a triumphal victory march. If one were to spell out the force of this image, it looks less like a *reconciliation* of the powers than their *defeat*. It may be that we should not press this distinction too far (theological metaphors may not always neatly cohere), or that the two can be made to fit if we regard 'making peace' as a kind of 'pacification' of the powers. Alternatively, the 'things in heaven' may be reconciled precisely by the defeat and destruction of 'rulers and powers' which have ruined the proper orientation of the heavenly world. Whatever is precisely in view (if indeed the author had a precise view of the matter), the important point is that the most powerful forces of disintegration and hostility in the universe have been dealt with decisively through the crucifixion and resurrection of Christ.

Yet here we run up against another paradox, in that the hymn is introduced by a reference to a 'power' (*exousia*) that seems to be still well-armed and undisgraced. In 1.13 God is acclaimed as rescuing believers from 'the power of darkness' and transferring them to the kingdom of his Son, and if such a rescue takes place, chronologically, after the victory of the cross, one wonders why this 'power' is still so powerful. Again, perhaps the point should not be pressed, since the victory depicted in 2.15 might not imply the annihilation of the powers, merely a devastating blow that makes possible the rescue of those once under their control. Theological metaphors do not translate neatly into systematic doctrines.

Nonetheless, there are some important ambiguities surrounding the topic of the 'powers' which call attention to some theological paradoxes inherent in Colossians. We may illustrate them most sharply by asking in what sense Christ is described in 2.10 as 'the head of every rule (*archē*) and power (*exousia*)'. Is he their 'head' inasmuch as they, together with the 'thrones and dominions', were created in him and for him (1.16)? Or is he their head by virtue of reconciling and/or pacifying them in his death and resurrection (1.20; 2.15)? In either case, there is a good reason to affirm Christ's supreme authority, but different grounds are offered for the basis and nature of that authority. Here again, the universal character of Christ's claim on the world and the particularity of the event of salvation are placed side by side without a neat resolution of their differences in perspective.

The reference to 'the power of darkness' (1.13) indicates that Colossians does not regard the world, even after the resurrection, as a harmonious and integrated phenomenon. Linguistically, we may note that the phrase 'all things' is always used in a positive sense in relation to entities created, held together, penetrated and reconciled by Christ (e.g. 1.16, 17, 18, 19; 3.11), while the term 'the world' (*kosmos*) is used either neutrally (1.6) or in a negative sense as that which is opposed to Christ or that to which believers have died (2.8, 20). If they are to regard themselves as no longer living 'in the world' (2.20), it is clear that *kosmos* has more than a physical sense, representing a structure of life alien to Christ. As we have just seen, 'rulers and powers' are ambiguous entities which can be viewed as created in Christ, or under his authority, or opposed to his rule. The tension set up by these various conceptions suggests that reality can be viewed under different aspects, sometimes as a unified, sometimes as a divided phenomenon. That aspect of the Colossian paradox will have to be reviewed again at the end of the discussion.

5. *Christ and the Church*. One of the most striking aspects of the 'hymn' in 1.15-20 is the reference to the church in 1.18. After a depiction of creation as made and sustained in Christ, it comes as something of a surprise to find the statement 'he is the head of the body, the church' (1.18), before any mention of salvation. As we noted in Chapter 4, many exegetes consider that the reference to the church has been inserted here by the author, postulating that 'the body' originally meant 'the cosmos'. Our concern here is with the theology of Colossians *as it now stands*, and the mention of the church here indicates the very significant place it holds within the letter. Although Christ is claimed to be the head

of every rule and power in 2.10, neither they nor the cosmos are referred to explicitly as his body: that designation is kept uniquely for the church, both in 1.18 and in 1.24 (cf. 3.15). In these cases the singular 'the church' (*ekklēsia*) indicates the totality of the Christian community, but elsewhere in the letter *ekklēsia* can be used with reference to local house meetings (4.15-16). Thus the author can view the local gatherings of believers within a perspective so broad that 'the church' is an integral aspect of the meaning and redemption of 'all things'.

If 'the church' has this broader role, that is only because of its special relationship to Christ. The body draws its nourishment, its growth and its unity from the head according to the special physiology of 2.19, and that means that the life of the community of believers is wholly dependent on the (risen) life of Christ. In relation to 'the world', Christian believers are dead—their life is 'hidden' with Christ in God (2.20; 3.3); to become a believer is thus to 'receive Christ Jesus' (2.6) and Christian existence remains 'rooted and built up in him' (another mixed metaphor, 2.7). But that means being connected to the very life-centre of the universe, the One who, as the 'first-born from the dead', is the origin and focus of the (new) creation (1.18). Thus it is not surprising that Christian initiation can be described as 'putting off the old humanity' and 'putting on the new', which is 'being renewed in knowledge according to the image of its creator' (3.9-10). Such language probably derives from the practice of baptism (with its disrobing and reclothing), but it also carries unmistakable echoes of Gen. 1.26-27. Here then, in the church, is not simply some new club or cultic association, nor merely an offshoot of Judaism, but the beginnings of a new humanity, the sign and seal of the new creation taking shape on earth, a body growing in the shape and with the energy of the renewed life of the universe. If it can be said that Christ is 'all in all' in relation to the church (3.11), it is here that the scope and potential of the 'hymn' is being put into effect.

These are enormous claims for a movement that in the first century constituted far less than 1 per cent of the population of the Roman empire, and even less in relation to the wider human race. Yet such boldness is of a piece with the claim that the Christ worshipped as the Lord and Life of Christian believers is the focal point of the whole creation. Whatever rules and regulations came before Christ (even those of Judaism) are the 'shadow' cast by the real substance (2.17), human culture finding not only its fulfilment but its deepest truths in him. Thus it can be claimed that those who belong to Christ are 'filled' (2.10), and the process of life and growth in Christ can be depicted as a path to 'perfection' or 'full maturity' (*teleiotes*, 1.28; 3.14; 4.12). The church is thus not some special grouping or small coterie of humanity, but humanity as it was designed to be, humanity at its fullest and highest potential.

6. *Christ and the Life of the Community.* The way Colossians describes the life of the church indicates how such stupendous claims can be entertained. A central activity of this renewed humanity is the exercise of thanks and praise. Thankfulness and joy are particularly prominent themes in our letter, found in the opening thanksgiving (1.3, 11-12), in the first appeal to the addressees (2.7), in the closing exhorations (4.2, omitted in one text) and, most importantly, in the specific instructions about church life (3.15-17). The repeated references here to thankfulness and gratitude are not simply some ploy to encourage a 'feel good factor'. They describe a community bound together and bound to God in what may be considered the highest human activity, the peak of human potential. Such worship of God is implicitly claimed to be far superior to the worship of (or with) angels referred to in 2.18 (see Chapter 3): it is superior because it is performed in the name of 'the Lord Jesus' (3.17), the head and unifying energy of creation.

Closely associated with thanksgiving is the unity and harmony of the community. It is notable that the virtues that the 'elect of God' are to put on in 3.12 all promote community welfare (while the vices of 3.8 cause the breakdown of relationships). The importance of communal peace is further emphasized in 3.13-15, where a premium is placed on forgiveness, forbearance and love. And it is not by accident that these are the qualities of the renewed humanity. The forgiveness that believers are to show mirrors the way in which they have been forgiven (3.13), that is, it embodies that reconciling power of Christ that can integrate the universe (1.20-22); such is 'the peace of Christ' that rules both 'in their hearts' and 'in the one body', that is, in the community of the church (3.17). Similarly, the love that constitutes the supreme clothing of the new humanity can be described as 'the bond of perfection', perhaps in the sense of 'the bond that brings about perfection' (3.14). For the Christian community to display love is not, therefore, to practise some private virtue or special habit: love is the means by which the true humanity reaches its highest potential. It is through such a bond that the whole body grows (cf. 1.4; 2.19), in contrast to the alienating and disintegrating effects of the 'philosophy' (2.16-18). And the 'bond of love' is surely part of that reunifying momentum of the new creation depicted in the second strophe of the 'hymn' (1.18b-20).

7. *Christ and the Hope of Glory.* If the community of believers thus anticipates in some sense the renewal and recreation of the whole universe, their life in Christ constitutes also their hope (1.27). The references to 'hope' in this letter sometimes place it spatially 'in the heavens' (1.5; cf. 3.1-4), and the predominant metaphors of salvation in Colossians are not so much to do with time (waiting for the future, looking from now to then) as with space (being raised, looking from below to above). This is clearly a result of the 'realized eschatology' of the letter, since the claim that believers are already raised with Christ (2.12-13; 3.1) lessens the sense of unfulfilled expectations and directs attention less 'forward' in time than 'up' in space, where the risen Christ already is and where also the believers' life may be said to be 'hidden with Christ in God' (3.2-3). That is not to say that there are no references to the future in Colossians, as for instance in 3.6 (the coming wrath) and 3.24 (receiving one's reward at the judgment). But there is no sense of immediate expectation in such references, nor do they indicate that a fundamental change of world conditions is expected. When Christ is 'revealed' (3.4), his disclosure is not said to effect any change beyond the revelation also of believers; indeed, it is hard to see how anything further could be kept for the future since the 'hymn' has suggested that a universal reconciliation has already taken place (1.20). Thus

the 'glory' hoped for is not (or at least, is not explicitly said to be) a new state of affairs or a further redemption (cf. Phil. 3.20-21; Rom. 8.18-25); nothing concrete is depicted beyond a revelation of the status and identity of 'the saints' (1.12; 3.4).

This way of viewing eschatology has had its effects on the anthropology of the letter. In the eschatology of Romans, salvation is celebrated but still crucially incomplete, since a resurrection of the body is yet to come (Rom. 8.11, 18-25; cf. 1 Cor. 15.35-58). In Colossians there is no qualification of the statement that believers are already raised (2.12-13), and thus no mention of a future resurrection body. It corresponds to this that salvation can be described as a metaphorical circumcision, a shedding of 'the body of flesh' (2.11). 'Flesh' is here not straightforwardly what we might call physical substance (2.18 can refer to a 'mind of flesh'), but the metaphor does suggest that salvation is primarily an inner reality. When the author bids his addressees to 'put to death the limbs which are of the earth' (3.5), he does not mean, of course, some physical mutilation, but the insistence that their true life is above rather than below (3.1-4) lessens to some degree their orientation towards the material realm. This is not a clear-cut 'Hellenistic' dualism between 'the soul' and 'the body' (note the positive 'bodily' in 2.9), but one might say that the realized eschatology of the letter has encouraged its anthropology to move a little along the spectrum in that direction. That fits also the emphasis we noted on 'wisdom' and 'knowledge'; if salvation consists in coming to 'know' a 'mystery' (Christ), there is less concern about the destiny of one's body and its material environment.

8. *Christ and Service in Everyday Life.* The above observations should not be taken to imply that Colossians regards the present everyday life of believers as insignificant. Although their orientation is on 'the things above', the sphere *in which* Christian obedience is fulfilled remains the everyday social and physical world. Indeed, it is in the present community of believers and in their daily lives that the reality of the new creation is brought to birth. Thus the comprehensiveness of the vision of Colossians is well expressed by the command that everything in word or deed should be performed 'in the name of the Lord Jesus' (3.17).

Where the philosophy demarcated taboo times and foods and operated according to merely human principles (2.16, 20-22), the Christian sphere of activity is as broad as all creation and is governed by the inner truth of that creation, Christ.

It is thus quite fitting that Colossians should be the occasion for the first occurrence of the 'household code' (3.18-4.1; see above, Chapter 4). Here we find the mundane relationships of daily life claimed for Christ and brought under the sway of his ultimate authority. The address to all parties, children included, indicates that Christ's 'all in all' (3.11) extends to every stage and status of life, and the repeated refrain of the code is that life should be lived 'in' or 'to' the Lord. This is particularly striking, and emphasized at length, in the exhortation to slaves (3.22-25). Many Christian slaves must have found themselves in slavery to non-Christian owners (cf. 1 Pet. 2.18-25) and it was natural for them to be dismayed that their lives were to be spent bringing benefit to 'outsiders' who were still in the 'power of darkness'. In such circumstances, the temptation to do the minimum necessary must have been strong. Colossians urges all Christian slaves to work their best, not simply from some sense of proper order, but because even slaves can understand their lives to be spent in the service of Christ. 'Whatever you do, work wholeheartedly as to the Master (Lord) and not to human masters' (3.23), for 'you are serving the Master Christ' (3.24). Slaves may well be treated unfairly (the 'wrongdoer' in 3.25 may refer to either master or slave), but the Christian slave can find even in such difficult circumstances a rationale and goal for life. Thus the code indicates how even the most unpromising circumstances in life can become an arena in which the mystery of Christ is recognized and served.

To us it is now somewhat scandalous that the code accepts and even 'sanctifies' relationships of subordination, altering the motives but hardly the basic character of household life in an exploitative and patriarchal society. More will be said on the practical options concerning slaves in our discussion of Philemon (Chapter 7), but for now we may note how the 'conservatism' of Colossians in this area is consonant with its whole theology. The claim that Christ is 'all in all' (3.11) certainly means that no sphere of life is left untouched by his claim and that everything is to be done in his name (3.17); all of life is thus integrated in the believers' devotion to the Lord. But their investments lie not in earthly things but in 'the things above', where Christ their life now lives (3.1-3). Christians may thus accept the status quo since it represents the circumstances *in which* they serve the Lord, but not *for which* they live. Their true life is hidden with Christ (3.3), so that slaves, for instance, can perform their duties as part of a hidden transaction in the service of Christ. That gives meaning to their slavery, but also reduces the incentive to change those circumstances. The upward movement of their devotion enables them to dedicate all their living to Christ, without needing to be unduly concerned by its favourable or unfavourable conditions. That perspective may have helped to dignify the quality of life in circumstances which were, in any case, outside the slave's control.

Universalism and Particularism in Dialectic

Although the theology of Colossians has been considered under eight separate headings, it is clear enough that the whole hangs together remarkably well. At every turn its focal point proves to be Christology, but the vision of Christ generated in the letter is impressively comprehensive, embracing all of creation, all time, all the 'powers' and all of life. Still, the letter is fashioned around a pervasive tension to which we may now return in conclusion.

On the one hand, we have observed the repeated note of universalism in the letter, where Christ is acclaimed as the centre and focus of 'all things'. *All* of creation came into existence in him and for him, and *all things* cohere in him. No power is before or beyond him, for he is the head of *every* rule and authority; moreover his death and resurrection effect the reconciliation of *all things*, both in heaven and on earth. Christ is the 'mystery' hidden through *all time*, in whom are found *all* the treasures of wisdom and knowledge. The confession of 3.11 could hardly be more apt: Christ is '*all things in all things*'. Here then the Christian faith stakes out its claim in the widest possible terms. It is no new-fangled or minority cult, pandering to the special interests of a small pocket of humanity. Its truth is not one truth among others, nor its Lord a recent arrival in a world of many competing gods. On the contrary, Colossians lays a Christian claim on the whole of life, the whole of humanity, the whole of history and the whole of the universe, all in the name of Christ, the secret of all things.

On the other hand, the letter portrays a range of dualisms, which emphasize in various respects the *particularism* of the church. Baptism stands as the point of entry into the church, the moment when the 'old humanity' is shed and the 'new humanity' is donned, with their hugely contrasting characteristics. It also marks the boundary between 'the power of darkness' and 'the kingdom of God's Son', effecting a 'rescue' without which there is only the prospect of God's wrath. In such a transaction, believers are brought from death to life and reconciled to a God from whom they are otherwise alienated. As Christians, they know themselves as the 'elect of God' and are distinguished from 'outsiders'. Even now they are presented with a choice between 'human teaching' and the wisdom of Christ, between 'the elemental things/spirits of the cosmos' and what is 'according to Christ'. The secret of Christ is not universally known and the true life of Christ is not universally diffused; only the church counts as the body of Christ and only those who believe in Christ can know his resurrection life.

Thus the universal and the particular stand in continual dialectic throughout Colossians and there seems no good reason to collapse one into the other. Although it is often claimed that the author edits and alters his 'hymnic' source in the direction of ecclesiology and particularity, only theological prejudice (against a 'mythological' or 'cosmic' Christology) can obliterate the universal dimensions of the letter. Even if at times the two elements in the theology of the letter appear to grate against one another, or leave us with paradox and ambiguity, we should allow for the possibility that that is a deliberate, even a necessary, state of affairs. Our author cannot be deprived of his claim that Christ is 'all in all', nor of his sense of entry into the secret of life through the radical change effected in baptism. To weaken either side of this dialectic would be to treat his theology with less seriousness than it deserves.

In fact, it might be claimed that the power of the tension represented by the theology of Colossians was crucial for the subsequent development of Christianity. On the one hand, the universal claims of the letter gave permission to the church to regard itself not as a private or self-enclosed entity with an incommunicable message, but as a potentially universal body which represented a new way of being human endowed with a message concerning the whole of 'reality'. Such a vision made Christian theology fertile enough to engage in all the moral, philosophical and metaphysical debates of its day, and figures like Justin, Clement, Origen and Irenaeus are heirs and exemplars of this phenomenon. At the same time, the sense of distinction represented by the particularism of the letter made the church robust enough to maintain its special identity, not allowing its theology to become dissipated in a general sense of 'universal good' nor letting its community lose its sharply differentiated profile. One cannot claim that Colossians had a unique influence in this regard, but it clearly lies behind the further reflections of Ephesians, and the two letters together had a considerable impact on early Christian thought. More generally, they represent a 'watershed' stage in which the early Christian movement came to terms with its international growth and explored the full potential of its belief in the risen Lord. That the author of Colossians was able to think creatively on this topic and to lay claim to the universe in the name of Christ, without dissolving the uniqueness of the Christian community, was a remarkable and highly significant achievement.

It is precisely this tension which may enrich the dialogue between Colossians and contemporary Christian theology. Undoubtedly, some aspects of Colossians seem to us awkward and unassimilable, not least the portrayal of unequal relations in the household code. Those who hold a low Christology, reckoning Christ merely a 'human individual' (Wedderburn, pp. 28-29), will also find the Christological claims of this letter somewhat absurd. The statements of the 'hymn' cannot be uttered 'coolly and rationally', but it is not clear that that disqualifies them as expressions of Christian faith (Wedderburn, pp. 66-71; contrast Lincoln, pp. 143-44 in the same volume). To gaze at the image of Christ as Cosmocrator in the central dome of a Greek Orthodox church is to sense something of what the Colossian hymn has meant to the church through the centuries, and post-Enlightenment Christians should not dispel that image too rapidly. Perhaps our knowledge of the cosmos and the imperfections inherent in nature makes us hesitate to interpret the claims of the Colossian hymn too literally (could they all be made as readily in relation to 'black holes' as in relation to stars?). But the underlying claim that in Christ is to be found the life and integrating power of the universe is not to be lightly abandoned.

More especially, the dialectic noted between the universal horizon of Colossians and its particular commitment to the church community may help to balance Christian theology in some of its present dilemmas. On the one hand, the universal dimension of Christian claims is not to be narrowed out of embarrassment in a pluralist culture or under the pressure of post-modern challenges to all-embracing truths. A retreat into self-inflicted marginality would neuter the power of the Colossian 'hymn', and the scope of its claim that Christ is 'all in all' serves as a powerful incentive for Christian engagement with the world, not least in a concern for 'the integrity of creation'. On the other hand, the particularity of faith in Christ should not be dissipated by a general notion of 'the universal spirit of Christ', through which the church is in danger of losing its ability to bear a distinctive witness; it must still face for itself, and present to others, the radical contrasts between the old and the new humanity. To preserve this balance and maintain this dialectic is arguably of crucial importance for the future of the church, and ecumenical debates will properly rage around its many inter-related facets. As noted in Chapter 1, Colossians has already had a significant role to play in those debates since the 1960s, and everything noted in this chapter indicates that it could continue to offer Christian theology a notable resource for some time to come.

Further Reading

The commentaries that offer the greatest engagement with the theology of the letter are those by Lohse, Pokorný, Schweizer and Wright. Note also:

Hoppe, R., *Der Triumph des Kreuzes: Studien zum Verhältnis des Kolosser-briefes zur paulinischen Kreuzestheologie* (Stuttgart: Katholisches Bibel-werk, 1994).

Käsemann, E., 'A Primitive Christian Baptismal Liturgy', in *Essays on New Testament Themes* (London: SCM Press, 1964), pp. 149-68.

Meeks, W.A., 'In One Body: The Unity of Humankind in Colossians and Ephesians', in J. Jervell and W.A. Meeks (eds.), *God's Christ and his People: Studies in Honour of Nils Alstrup Dahl* (Oslo: Universitets-forlaget, 1977), pp. 209-21.

Merklein, H., 'Paulinische Theologie in der Rezeption des Kolosser- und Epheserbriefes', in *idem, Studien zu Jesus und Paulus* (Tübingen: Mohr [Paul Siebeck], 1987), pp. 409-47.

Wedderburn, A.J.M. and A.T. Lincoln, *The Theology of the Later Pauline Epistles* (Cambridge: Cambridge University Press, 1993).

6

THE LETTER TO PHILEMON: STORY AND STRATEGY

The letter to Philemon is to my mind the most intriguing and
beguiling of all Paul's letters, with its teasing historical allusions and its special rhetorical charms. The questions we face
here are rather different from those that have concerned us
in relation to Colossians. In the case of Philemon we need
spend no time discussing its authorship, since nowadays
even the most suspicious critics willingly attribute it to Paul.
F.C. Baur once argued for the possibility that the letter be
considered a spurious fiction, designed to illustrate a general
principle of reconciliation; but his suggestion is now rightly
dismissed. The way our text alludes to people and events
clearly familiar to writer and addressee indicates that it is a
real letter, but it is this very allusiveness that creates the
greatest difficulties for us who read this personal correspondence nearly two thousand years later. We sense here, even
more than in relation to Colossians, that we need to reconstruct the story underlying the letter before we can properly
appreciate its strategies and goals. Once again, *something*
might be salvaged of literary and theological interest even if
we were totally ignorant of the life-setting of this letter, but
it is so immediate and specific that it entices us to attempt to
reconstruct the events and relationships it reflects. This,
then, will be our first point of entry.

The Story behind the Letter

Discerning the story behind this letter is not an easy task. Paul appears to be in prison; but where and under what conditions? He writes chiefly to Philemon (others are named as well in v. 2, but the bulk of the letter is addressed to 'you' singular); but what has brought the two into contact and what previous relationship have they enjoyed? The third principal figure in the letter is Onesimus, who appears to be Philemon's slave; but what was their previous history and how did Onesimus relate to the church in Philemon's house (v. 2)? We are given some clues by the notice that Onesimus was formerly considered 'useless' (v. 11) and by the indication of some wrong or debt between Onesimus and Philemon (vv. 18-19), but much is still obscure. Finally, Onesimus appears to be present with Paul at the time of writing, but how did he come to be there and what has he been doing of service to Paul (v. 13)?

Some of these questions are unanswerable, since our only evidence is the letter itself and it simply will not respond to all our queries. (If Colossians is authentic, the reference to Onesimus in 4.9 adds a further fragment of evidence, but hardly of much value for these questions; if it is pseudonymous, the reference is probably fictional and adds nothing at all.) However, most scholars think we have just enough evidence to piece together a plausible story. Ever since our earliest known interpreters, the dominant consensus has been that Onesimus has run away from Philemon's house, has encountered Paul and been converted by him, and is now being sent back with this letter to face his aggrieved master, Philemon. Within this consensus, opinions have differed chiefly on two questions: (a) the nature of the wrong and/or debt alluded to in v. 18 (is this some misdemeanour before Onesimus ran away, a theft at the time he absconded, or the damage he has inflicted by being away?); and (b) the means by which Onesimus came to encounter Paul (was he arrested and put in the same prison, was he taken to Paul by mutual friends, or did he seek Paul out deliberately?). But these have been comparatively minor disagreements within the framework of the consensus that Onesimus is away without his master's permission and that Paul now has the delicate task of reconciling a runaway slave with his owner.

In recent years, this consensus has been questioned from a number of angles, since it clearly depends on inferences that are not all self-evident. For instance, there is no reference in the letter to Onesimus running away: v. 15 says only that 'he was separated from you for a while'. Are we required to give this the sinister interpretation of the runaway hypothesis, or will other hypotheses fit equally well? And is it certain that Onesimus is being returned with this letter, or is Paul merely writing about Onesimus, seeking permission to keep him at his side (vv. 13-14)? It has even been questioned whether Onesimus is Philemon's slave, since the latter is nowhere said to be his master. Such challenges helpfully force us to re-examine the consensus and test whether it rests on a secure basis.

The last named question, whether Onesimus is Philemon's slave, can be answered relatively simply. Callahan argues that the reference to 'slave' in v. 16 is purely metaphorical, and that Onesimus was Philemon's literal brother who had also now become a Christian ('a beloved brother, both in the flesh and in the Lord'). However, the wording of the phrase 'no longer as a slave but as more than a slave' (v. 16) clearly suggests that a literal slave status is in view, as is confirmed by the way Paul asks Philemon's permission for what Onesimus is to do, and suggests he could serve Paul on Philemon's behalf (vv. 13-14). Thus we may place Onesimus securely among Philemon's slaves, though v. 11 suggests that he was not highly regarded by his master.

The first two questions, whether Onesimus has run away and whether he is being returned with this letter, may be taken together and are much more complex. John Knox, who wrote an intriguing book on Philemon (see Further Reading), considered it uncertain whether Onesimus was a runaway, and argued that Paul was here only referring his case to Philemon, not sending him back; indeed Knox insisted that the whole point of the letter was the request to keep Onesimus as his associate. This argument has been developed by some other scholars (e.g. Winter and Wansink), who argue that Onesimus was no runaway but had been sent to

Paul by Philemon's church, bearing some aid. Thus the letter is not a plea for reconciliation, but a note of thanks for that gift and a request that Onesimus be allowed to remain serving Paul's needs in prison, released from his duties at home. It is certainly fair to point out that there is no reference to Onesimus running away, and that the opening thanksgiving (vv. 4-7) makes no mention of any such difficulty. However, the consensus theory can explain these silences easily enough (Paul was being exceptionally tactful), and this alternative thesis itself faces two major obstacles. In the first place, it has to give an unlikely meaning to the verbs in vv. 12 and 15 usually translated 'sending him back' and 'have him back'; thus on linguistic grounds the Knox–Winter thesis is very shaky and the text is clear enough that Onesimus is really accompanying this letter. Secondly, Onesimus hardly seems the sort of person to have been commissioned by a church to take a gift to Paul. According to the birth metaphor in v. 10, Onesimus has become a Christian only after encountering Paul in prison, and v. 11 acknowledges that he was previously considered 'useless' by Philemon. Moreover, Paul's admission that Onesimus may have wronged his master (v. 18) suggests that some real grievance had arisen between them. Would Philemon's church employ a 'useless' non-Christian slave, in bad odour with his master, for an important service to Paul?

Thus the balance of probability lies against the revisionist reconstructions just outlined. The evidence we have just considered, together with the extremely careful way Paul piles on his charm, points towards some serious breakdown in the relationship between Onesimus and Philemon. The benign 'he was separated from you' (v. 15) can be taken as a euphemistic way of describing a parting neither planned nor wished by Philemon. Are we then driven back to the traditional 'runaway' hypothesis, or are there other possible explanations for this parting?

The main difficulty in the 'runaway' thesis lies in explaining how Onesimus came to be with Paul. Most runaways tried to 'disappear', understandably enough, and it seems odd for a runaway to identify himself by going to one of his master's associates! Onesimus's encounter with Paul has sometimes been taken to be accidental, by means of his incarceration in the same prison. But the two prisoners would not be kept in the same conditions, and if he were caught and imprisoned Onesimus would be sent back by the magistrates, not by Paul. Since a runaway might seek a place of asylum (from which Roman law allowed that a slave could either be reconciled to his owner or sold to another), some scholars have toyed with the idea that Onesimus might regard Paul's location as a place of asylum (see Goodenough), but it is hard to see how this could legally be so. The most likely solution on the runaway hypothesis is that, having fled with the intention to hide, Onesimus has had second thoughts and has come to Paul hoping that he will intercede for him with Philemon. Although Paul would be in a precarious position legally if he harboured the runaway Onesimus, this solution is not impossible, particularly if Onesimus's stay with Paul was brief.

However, another and in some ways neater solution has commended itself to many scholars recently (see e.g. Lampe, Rapske, Bartchy and Dunn's commentary). On this hypothesis, Onesimus has got into trouble with Philemon and has left his master's house specifically to find Paul, who, as a friend of his master, will have the necessary influence to intercede for him. The only difference from the version of the runaway hypothesis just outlined is that, in this case, Onesimus's quest for Paul was not 'second thoughts' but his primary intention. And, according to Roman jurists, a slave who left his master's property in quest of an advocate, intending to return to his master, was not technically to be considered a 'runaway' (*fugitivus*). On either hypothesis, Onesimus is clearly in difficulty with Philemon, but if he deliberately sought Paul out, Philemon might not have the extra grievance that his slave had, technically speaking, run away.

This may, indeed, be the most satisfactory explanation of events, though we might have expected Paul to reassure Philemon about Onesimus's intentions, since, in the absence of his slave, Philemon's first assumption would be that he had run away (it was a common tactic for slaves). We should also note that the jurists' distinction between a 'runaway' and a slave who absconded to gain help from an advocate may not have counted for much in popular perceptions. Amidst the Roman legal opinions cited by proponents of this hypothesis we find the observation that 'the ignorant' generally take any slave who stays away for a night (without permission) to be a fugitive (Justinian, *Digest* 21.1.17.5). Thus the technical distinctions drawn by Roman jurists may not correspond to common presumptions, according to which slaves were not to be trusted and any absenteeism was likely to be given the worst construction. Thus it is a moot point how much Roman law has to do with the realities of social prejudice, especially (in this case) among ordinary provincials in Asia Minor.

However, if we follow this hypothesis of Onesimus's deliberate quest for Paul, and if we assume that Paul and Philemon took the 'enlightened' view of the jurists on this matter, then Onesimus's situation was not quite as grave as the 'runaway' hypothesis usually suggests. He has clearly fallen out badly with Philemon (that is why he has come to Paul), but his return will not be quite as shamefaced as the return of a runaway, since he could claim that he always intended to come back; correspondingly, Philemon was entitled to punish him for his previous misdemeanours, but not for 'flight'. A slave in Onesimus's position would naturally seek out an advocate with maximum leverage over his master, and this would be true of Paul only inasmuch as he was Philemon's fellow Christian, indeed the one through whom Philemon became a Christian (so v. 19 implies). Thus the non-Christian Onesimus has come to Paul precisely because of Paul's Christian identity and influence, and in this situation it is hardly surprising that he himself became a Christian (v. 10). The suspicious might wonder whether Onesimus reckoned, shrewdly, that becoming a believer would be to his advantage, both in getting Paul on his side and in winning a better reception from Philemon!

Whatever Onesimus's motives, Paul has clearly accepted a role as his advocate, and now writes to Philemon to bring about some reconciliation and to put their relationship on a better footing for the future. We may thus now turn to consider the letter itself.

The Strategy of the Letter

A key aspect of Paul's letter is the way he represents what has happened, portraying the actors and the events from the perspective, and in the order, that will best suit his appeal (see Petersen, chapter 1). Thus it is noticeable that Onesimus is not mentioned until v. 10, after much also has already been said in praise of Philemon, that his coming to Paul is referred to only as a 'separation' from Philemon for a while (v. 15), and that reference to the 'wrong' he has done is left until near the end of the letter (v. 18) and then put into a conditional clause ('if he has wronged you in any way...'). Indeed, the letter to Philemon has always fascinated careful readers, who have noted the techniques of 'holy flattery' (Luther) by which Paul butters up his friend. The address to 'our dear friend and co-worker' (v. 1) is followed by a carefully phrased thanksgiving (vv. 4-7) at pains to praise Philemon for his love and his 'refreshment of the hearts of the saints', compliments that Paul will subsequently 'cash in' for the sake of his appeal for Onesimus (vv. 12, 20). There are also many other ways in which Paul applies pressure (see further the analysis by Church). The whole of Philemon's house church is addressed at the start of the letter, thus ensuring that Philemon is answerable to more than just the absent Paul. Paul's request is presented as an appeal rather than a command on two occasions (vv. 8, 14), but each time the more brutal alternative is mentioned as a none-too-subtle indication of the hierarchical relationship between Paul and Philemon; the closing reference to 'obedience' finally makes that quite clear (v. 21). Perhaps the subtlest move of the letter comes in vv. 18-19, where Paul refers to Onesimus's wrongdoing as a debt, then takes it upon himself (with a hand-written commitment to pay, v. 19a), and then overturns it altogether by alluding to the debt that Philemon owes to him (v. 19b). Here 'I say nothing about' is a well-known rhetorical device, a way of mentioning something when making out you are not going to do so. Enough is said here to indicate that Paul's role in Philemon's conversion (interpreted as resulting in a debt to Paul, not to God) should be taken fully into account, making quite insignificant whatever

Onesimus/Paul now owes. Thus Philemon is turned from creditor to debtor in the space of two verses, and loaded with a debt so large ('your very self') that he is under limitless obligation to Paul. The 'casual' request for a guest-room at the end of the letter (v. 22) indicates that Paul will come to see how that obligation is being fulfilled!

There is one feature of the letter, however, which seems at first sight very curious, and that is the lack of reference to Onesimus's remorse. As we have seen, this cannot be explained by saying Onesimus had nothing to be sorry for, since, even if he did not technically run away, there has clearly been a serious rupture in his relationship with Philemon. The 'if' in v. 18 can hardly mean that Paul does not know whether a wrong has been committed: he would hardly mention this possibility unless it were an obstacle to Onesimus's rehabilitation. Nor can it be taken to suggest that Paul doubts whether Onesimus is really at fault (so Dunn); his job is not to adjudicate but to appeal, and he is not in a position to contest Philemon's judgment on the matter. Nor is it enough simply that Onesimus returns: Philemon needs to know on what basis he does so. Would it not have been natural and effective for Paul to mention Onesimus's repentance?

That it would indeed have been natural for Paul to appeal to Philemon on this basis is made clear from some letters written by Pliny (c. 61/62–113 CE) in a situation very similar to Paul's. In two letters Pliny writes to a friend, Sabinianus, concerning a freedman (former slave) who had offended his patron (former owner) and had come to Pliny specifically for his advocacy. Thus this is precisely an example of 'resort to a friend of the master', which we found to be a plausible explanation of the Onesimus story, the only difference being that Pliny's case concerns a freedman (under continuing obligations to his former master) while Onesimus is a slave. But the similarity of situation only makes more striking the difference in the strategy that Pliny and Paul adopt. It will be helpful here to quote Pliny in full:

> To Sabinianus. The freedman of yours with whom you said you were angry has been to me, flung himself at my feet, and clung to me as if I were you. He begged my help with many tears, though

he left a good deal unsaid; in short, he convinced me of his genuine penitence. I believe he has reformed, because he realizes he did wrong. You are angry, I know, and I know too that your anger was deserved, but mercy wins most praise when there was just cause for anger. You loved the man once, and I hope you will love him again, but it is sufficient for the moment if you allow yourself to be appeased. You can always be angry again if he deserves it, and will have more excuse if you were once placated. Make some concession to his youth, his tears and your own kind heart, and do not torment him or yourself any longer—anger can only be a torment to your gentle self.

I'm afraid you will think I am using pressure, not persuasion, if I add my prayers to his—but this is what I shall do, and all the more freely and fully because I have given the man a very severe scolding and warned him firmly that I will never make such a request again. This was because he deserved a fright, and is not intended for your ears; for maybe I *shall* make another request and obtain it, as long as it is nothing unsuitable for me to ask and you to grant (*Letter* 9.21; trans. Betty Radice, Loeb Classical Library).

A little later, Pliny writes another letter expressing his satisfaction that his first has been heeded:

To Sabinianus. You have done the right thing in taking back into your home and favour the freedman who was once dear to you, with my letter to mediate between you both. You will be glad of this, and I am certainly glad, first because I see you are willing to be reasonable and take advice when angry, and then because you have paid me the tribute of bowing to my authority, or, if you prefer, granting my request. So accept my compliments as well as my thanks, but, at the same time, a word of advice for the future: be ready to forgive the faults of your household even if there is no one there to intercede for them (*Letter* 9.24, Loeb Classical Library).

The most illuminating way to compare Pliny and Paul is to examine the way they present their relationships to the main parties involved. In each case the author writes to the aggrieved party on behalf of a social inferior, and their tactics are close enough to be comparable but different enough to indicate a fundamental distinction in their approach. We may consider their strategies under three headings:

1. *Stance towards the Aggrieved Party.* Pliny's approach to Sabinianus is that of a social superior who offers moral advice and expects his will to be followed. No doubt the freedman came to Pliny precisely because he was in a position to

exercise authority over Sabinianus, and Pliny performs that role extremely well. He pronounces moral platitudes ('mercy wins most praise when there was just cause for anger'), but a key point of his appeal lies in the insinuation that Sabinianus can maintain his moral reputation (for a 'kind heart' and 'gentleness') only if he acts as Pliny requires. Pliny's social superiority is also evident in the candid recognition that to add his prayers to those of the freedman would be 'using pressure, not persuasion'—which he then proceeds to do! The subsequent letter of congratulation (9.24) reaffirms this hierarchical relationship, by thanking Sabinianus for granting Pliny's requests and complimenting him for obeying his authority. By such obedience Sabinianus has fulfilled his proper role in the social hierarchy of Roman society: he has not demeaned himself by pardoning an inferior (his freedman), because his action represents his fitting submission to a superior (Pliny).

Paul's approach to Philemon contains some of the same characteristics. He too has been approached by Onesimus precisely because he is in a position to influence Philemon, and if he were to write a letter without utilizing any of the authority at his disposal he would be failing in his responsibilities to Onesimus. Rather like Pliny, Paul makes explicit the alternatives he could adopt—he could command, or he could merely appeal (vv. 8, 13-14). Unlike Pliny he makes a point of forgoing his right to command on the basis of love, but in fact by the end of the letter he is issuing direct commands (v. 20) and is confident of Philemon's 'obedience' (v. 21). Even if Philemon is to Paul 'a brother' (v. 7), 'a dear friend and a fellow worker' (v. 1), Paul has to make clear *some* grounds on which Philemon will not lose face by receiving Onesimus back in a friendly manner. As in Pliny's case, this is possible if Philemon can understand himself to be yielding to a superior. While in worldly terms Paul may well have been Philemon's social inferior, Paul's authority lies in the Christian sphere that Philemon has newly entered. Although he never refers to himself as an apostle, Paul's special role as messenger of the gospel is made clear in the repeated references to his imprisonment (vv. 1, 9, 10, 13, 23), and, most pertinently, in the reference to his unique role in

Philemon's conversion (v. 19). We have already noted how this turns Philemon in an instant from creditor to debtor, but the fact that the debt is owed to *Paul* is what gives this letter such moral and spiritual authority. In vv. 13-14 Paul simply takes it for granted that Philemon will recognize his responsibility to serve Paul, even if only indirectly by means of Onesimus.

2. *Stance towards the Miscreant.* At this point the strategies adopted by Pliny and Paul diverge radically. Pliny's attitude to the freedman is consistently aloof and condescending. It is notable that the freedman is never named, and is referred to at the beginning as '*your* freedman' (not anything to do with 'me'). Although Pliny can appeal to the fact that Sabinianus once had affection for the man, he shows none of his own. Pliny never ventures to disagree with Sabinianus in his judgment on the man ('I know that your anger was deserved') and suggests that his concern is just as much for Sabinianus's psychological equilibrium as for the fate of the freedman. The closest Pliny gets to the freedman in terms of common feeling is in 'adding my prayers to his', but the end of the first letter indicates the social distance that Pliny has preserved: he has given the man a 'very severe scolding' and frightened him by threatening never to interpose again. By indicating something different to Sabinianus (that he would intervene again if there were good reason to do so), Pliny shows that his discourse with the freedman has been condescendingly dishonest: it is good for the freedman to hear such threats even if they are not strictly true.

Paul's presentation of Onesimus is startlingly different. As soon as he is introduced he is named (v. 10) and presented to Philemon not as 'your slave' but as 'my son'. While Paul regularly refers to Christians as children of God, this is one of the few occasions in his letters where the relationship between converter and converted is described as that of parent to child (cf. Gal. 4.19; 1 Thess. 2.11); such terms are used here to express the closest possible bond between the two. Indeed as soon as he refers to sending Onesimus back, Paul describes him as 'my own heart' (v. 12)—an expression that he will make use of later (v. 20). Indeed, his own investment in Onesimus's welfare is indicated at every point where Paul describes Onesimus in relation to his master: he is now useful 'both to you and to me' (v. 11), he might be of service to Paul 'on your behalf' (v. 13), and he is to be regarded now as a beloved brother 'especially to me but how much more to you' (v. 16). At every point Paul interposes himself into the relationship between Philemon and Onesimus, and this strategy reaches its climax in the direct appeal of v. 17: 'if you consider me your partner (*koinōnos*), welcome him as you would welcome me'. Here is the essence of Paul's strategy: so to identify himself with Onesimus, and Onesimus with himself, that Philemon has to regard the returning Onesimus as if he were Paul himself. As a practical expression of this identification Paul offers to pay Onesimus's debt (vv. 18-19), and it is thus clear by the end that when Paul asks Philemon to 'refresh my heart' (v. 20; cf. v. 7), he is referring to Onesimus himself (the verb in v. 20a also puns on Onesimus's name). Thus the returning Onesimus is totally transformed in the eyes of his master: not only is he no longer useless, but now useful (v. 11), not only is he to be received 'no longer as a slave, but more than a slave, a beloved brother' (v. 16), he is now in an important sense no longer Onesimus, but Paul himself! The social distance that Pliny carefully preserved has been so reduced in this case as to be obliterated altogether.

3. *The Grounds for the Expected Reconciliation.* The difference we have just noted in their presentation of the miscreants has an important effect on the ways Pliny and Paul put forward their reasons for expecting a reconciliation between the hostile parties. Pliny makes the grounds for his appeal the circumstances of the offence, the character of Sabinianus and, above all, the repentance of the offender. Among the mitigating circumstances are the fact that the freedman is young ('make some concession to his youth'), was once well liked by Sabinianus ('you loved the man once') and that this is, apparently, the first offence: he has certainly been warned that he must never do the same again. Pliny also makes much of Sabinianus's moral character, his 'mercy', 'kind heart' (*indulgentia*) and gentle nature: it thus befits him to forgive in these circumstances. But the first and most powerful ground for appeal is the penitence of the freedman:

his submission, his tears and his consciousness of guilt have all given proof of his repentance (*paenitentia*) and convinced Pliny that he is reformed (*emendatus*). On these grounds it would seem reasonable to forgive the man, though a further important factor may be revealed in the final sentence of the first letter, where Pliny suggests that this is (and others in the future may also be) the sort of offence about which it is 'proper' (*deceat*) for him to appeal and for Sabinianus to forgive. Thus the resolution of this case will fit the framework of that moral code which Pliny and Sabinianus seek to uphold.

In comparison with Pliny, Paul's letter on behalf of Onesimus is striking in its failure to mention most of these obvious grounds for appeal. Paul does make some appeal to Philemon's moral character (his love for all the saints and his record of refreshing their hearts, vv. 4-7), but nothing is said here about extenuating circumstances or the propriety of forgiving such an offence, and no reference is made to Onesimus's repentance. Now it could be that there were no extenuating circumstances to which Paul could appeal, and that Onesimus was not truly repentant, but it is more likely that Paul's silence on these matters is because he feels he is on stronger ground pursuing a quite different argumentative strategy. As we have seen, a key element in that strategy is Paul's willingness to identify himself with Onesimus, so that the really important question for Philemon is not how he will regard a sorrowful slave but how he will treat Paul, his friend and father in the faith. Onesimus's debt will be repaid not by his repentance but by Paul, and that, as we have seen, is easily turned over into Philemon's debt to Paul. And the main reason that Paul can so identify himself with Onesimus is that the slave has become a new person by becoming a Christian. Although Paul remarks that Onesimus is now for the first time 'useful' (v. 11; his name means precisely that), the really essential thing about Onesimus is not that he is a reformed character (evidenced by his repentance) but that he is a 'beloved brother' (evidenced by his faith). This is the force of vv. 15-16 where the emphasis is on Onesimus's return as a *different person*, or rather as a person now to be regarded quite differently—'no longer as a slave, but as more than a slave, a beloved brother'. We shall have to see (in the next chapter) what might be implied by such a phrase, but what is important for us now is to note that it is this *category change* which Paul expects to make all the difference, not the evidence or promise of some moral improvement. This is clearly a powerful gambit on Paul's part, but one he could use only once and only in special circumstances. If Onesimus had not become a Christian, Paul would have had to write quite differently (if he had written at all). And if Onesimus had been a Christian before he left Philemon's house, Paul would not have been able to make his appeal on quite these terms. It is because Onesimus has *changed* while he has been away from Philemon that Paul can present him in this manner—changed not just in moral character but in identity. If in the future, as a Christian, Onesimus were to commit another such offence and flee to Paul again, Paul could not simply rewrite this letter (as Pliny could clearly rewrite much of what he wrote to Sabinianus). That is not to say that Paul could not find other grounds on which to bring about a reconciliation between Christians (cf. 1 Cor. 6.1-8; 2 Cor. 2.5-11), but it is to indicate the very special form of argumentation employed here, one that places all the stress on the utter difference caused by the event of becoming a Christian.

This sense of the category difference between Christians and non-Christians is replicated elsewhere in Paul (e.g. 1 Cor. 5.9–6.6), and the notion of conversion as a complete new beginning is, of course, in line with Pauline theology in other letters. 'If anyone is in Christ, there is a new creation' (2 Cor. 5.17), or, as Colossians puts it, baptism entails putting off the 'old humanity' (or 'old person') and putting on the new (Col. 3.9-11). In the case of Philemon, the 'old/new' language is not used, but Onesimus is regarded simply as having been 'born' (v. 10, not 'reborn'), just as Philemon owes to Paul his very self (*seauton*, v. 19). In a sense, then, what is brought about in conversion is not an entry into a new reality, but a discovery of the only true reality (cf. Petersen, p. 62). So powerful is this sense of the real that it threatens to reduce 'ordinary realities' to insignificance as a shadow world of no ultimate significance for the Christian. But what will this mean for Onesimus? The fact that he is now a Christian slave makes this question acute. Will his new status as 'beloved brother' render his social position as slave simply irrelevant, so that it should be of no concern to him or to other Christians that he carries on living as a slave? Or will the fact that he and his master are now 'brothers' to each other change the character of their relationship on the level of everyday social interaction, and is that change compatible with their continuing to live as master and slave? In the case of Pliny's letter, we know precisely on what basis the repentant freedman returns to his obligations: shamefaced, perhaps, and rather more cautious in the future, but otherwise carrying on much as before. But Paul has presented Onesimus as having undergone such a major change in identity that we are bound to ask what happens next. Is his slave status simply made irrelevant by his 'birth', so that it remains a matter of purely external significance for his enjoyment of his new (inner) life? Or will his new 'brother' relationship to Philemon alter his social conditions and expectations? Such are the questions we must consider in the following chapter.

Further Reading

For Commentaries on Philemon, see the list at the end of Chapter 1; most comment on the issues discussed here. See also:

Barclay, J.M.G., 'Paul, Philemon and the Dilemma of Christian Slave-Ownership', *NTS* 37 (1991), pp. 161-86.
Bartchy, S.S., 'Philemon, Epistle to', *ABD*, V, pp. 305-10.
Callahan, A.D., 'Paul's Epistle to Philemon: Toward an Alternative *Argumentum*', *HTR* 86 (1993), pp. 357-76.
Church, F.F., 'Rhetorical Structure and Design in Paul's Letter to Philemon', *HTR* 71 (1978), pp. 17-33.
Goodenough, E.R., 'Paul and Onesimus', *HTR* 22 (1929), pp. 181-83.
Knox, J., *Philemon among the Letters of Paul* (London: Collins, 1960).
Lampe, P., 'Keine "Sklavenflucht" des Onesimus', *ZNW* 76 (1985), pp. 135-37.
Nordling, J.G., 'Onesimus Fugitivus: A Defense of the Runaway Slave Hypothesis in Philemon', *JSNT* 41 (1991), pp. 97-119.
Petersen, N.R., *Rediscovering Paul: Philemon and the Sociology of Paul's Narrative World* (Philadelphia: Fortress Press, 1985).
Rapske, B.M., 'The Prisoner Paul in the Eyes of Onesimus', *NTS* 37 (1991), pp. 187-203.

Wansink, C.S., *Chained in Christ: The Experience and Rhetoric of Paul's Imprisonments* (JSNTSup, 130; Sheffield: Sheffield Academic Press, 1996), esp. pp. 175-99.

Winter, S.C., 'Paul's Letter to Philemon', *NTS* 33 (1987), pp. 1-15.

7

THE LETTER TO PHILEMON:
OUTCOME AND EVALUATION

The Outcome of the Letter

At the end of the last chapter we asked what were the implications of this letter as far as Onesimus's future was concerned, that is, whether or how Paul's presentation of Onesimus's new identity would affect his social status and his relationship to Philemon. Clearly the letter cannot tell us what actually happened when Onesimus returned home (and we have no sequel as in Pliny's second letter to Sabinianus), but if we could discern more precisely what Paul was asking Philemon to do, we might be able to say what would have happened if Philemon had bowed to Paul's pressure. Unfortunately, it is precisely when we start to ask what Paul is asking Philemon to do that the letter becomes most difficult to interpret. In pursuing this enquiry we need to undertake careful exegesis of the details of the text; but we must also keep a firm grasp on the realities of slavery in the Graeco-Roman world. Inevitably, also, many interpreters will be influenced by their own theological perspective on the relationship between Christianity and social change. This latter issue will concern us directly in the second part of this chapter, but it is worth noting already as it probably plays some part in the exegetical options that scholars adopt.

What, then, was Paul asking Philemon to do? If the letter finished at v. 14, there would be little difficulty in answering this question. Paul makes it tolerably clear in vv. 13-14 that, while he is sending Onesimus back at the moment, he really wants to keep him, 'so that he might be of service to me in your place during my imprisonment for the gospel' (v. 13).

Verse 14 indicates that Paul wanted Philemon's permission for this, but the 'good deed' mentioned there, which he wants to be 'voluntary and not something forced', clearly refers to letting Onesimus assist Paul. Since it was perfectly natural for a slave-owner to 'second' a slave to the service of another (usually a relative or friend), there is no reason, thus far in the letter, to think that Onesimus will perform this service other than as a continuing slave of Philemon. In any case, Paul is not expecting to be in prison for very long (cf. v. 22), so this arrangement is hardly permanent.

It is the following verses, however, that complicate the picture. There Paul describes the 'separation' of Philemon and Onesimus as 'for a while', with the purpose that 'you might have him back for ever, no longer as a slave but as more than a slave, a beloved brother—especially to me but how much more to you, both in the flesh and in the Lord' (vv. 15-16). Then, as noted, Paul issues his direct appeal on the basis of his 'partnership' with Philemon: 'welcome him as you would welcome me' (v. 17). There are two respects in which these verses ruin the clarity of the earlier instructions:

1. In the first place, it is now made slightly uncertain whether Paul wants Onesimus to come back, or whether he is more concerned about his reception by, and relationship to, Philemon. 'That you might have him back for ever' sounds like a permanent residence in Philemon's house, unless we take the 'have him back' in a non-physical sense (like 'regaining' a friend), with the 'for ever' pointing to a transcendent reality (Onesimus will be a fellow believer for eternity). Uncertain on this issue, some commentators conclude that Paul's concern in these verses is only with Onesimus's initial reception in Philemon's house ('welcome him as you would me, then send him back'), while others think that vv. 13-14 and vv. 15-17 represent two different options, either of which Paul would be happy to see Philemon follow.

2. Secondly, the verses we have just cited (vv. 15-17), together with the offer to pay Onesimus's debt (vv. 18-19) and the open-ended 'knowing that you will do even more than I say' (v. 21), raise the question whether Paul is content

that Onesimus simply carry on as Philemon's slave, being now also his 'brother'. Does he now hint (or even demand) that the 'brother' status should supplant that of slave, that is, that Philemon should give Onesimus his freedom? Much hinges here on the meaning of 'no longer as a slave but as more than a slave, a beloved brother' (for details see the commentaries and Barclay, pp. 170-86). The majority of commentators have taken this phrase to indicate only a spiritual change in the relationship between Philemon and Onesimus. Thus Caird comments, 'Paul is not concerned with the legal status of the slave, since this is transcended in the new relationship that makes all Christians equal members in the one family of God' (p. 222). Lohse (p. 203) and O'Brien (pp. 296-97) cite a comment by von Soden that the word 'as' (*hōs*) in v. 16 ('as a slave') 'expresses the subjective evaluation of the relationship without calling its objective form into question'. Of those that follow this interpretation of v. 16, some take the comment in v. 21 about Philemon doing 'even more than I say' as equally devoid of social significance for Onesimus: Lohse (p. 206) and O'Brien (pp. 305-306) this time cite Dibelius (revised by Greeven): 'the legal side of the matter is not in view at all'. Others, however, regard v. 21 as rather more suggestive than v. 16, with a hint, or at least a possible hint, at Onesimus's manumission (the technical term for freeing a slave); Lightfoot thus comments that 'throughout this epistle the idea [of manumission] seems to be present to his thought, though the word never passes his lips' (p. 345).

On the other side, a minority of commentators have found even in v. 16 an indication that Paul expects Philemon to manumit Onesimus. Bruce is the most confident: 'He writes as one who assumes that Philemon will do the decent thing—that he will take legal steps to change the master–slave relationship' (p. 217). This interpretation has also been followed in the full-length discussion by Petersen, who maintains that the equality implied by the relationship of brother to brother is incompatible with the disparity between master and slave, and that Paul expects the new relationship to supersede the old (see also Elliott, pp. 40-52). Finally, some scholars have regarded the statement in v. 16 as simply ambiguous, with the potential to be taken in either way (e.g. Stuhlmacher, Dunn). In this case, Paul might be deliberately opening a variety of options for Philemon, hoping that he will take his own decision in the light of the circumstances and in line with the demands of love.

I have argued elsewhere (see Further Reading) that the ambiguity in these instructions may be due to the fact that, for practical reasons, Paul did not know what to recommend. If we think about the practicalities of either option, there are obvious difficulties entailed for a slave-owner like Philemon. For instance, if he were to manumit Onesimus because he had now become a Christian, he would have to do the same for any other slaves who were already Christians, or who would (rather soon!) follow suit. It was certainly quite common for masters to manumit their slaves, but only after they had performed many years of service and, usually, at a price that enabled the master to purchase a substitute. But if there was a general sense that it was inappropriate for Christians to own Christian slaves, and if it was easy enough for slaves to become Christians, Philemon (and other Christian slave-owners) would find themselves unable to own any slaves at all. In the ancient world, such was the breadth of dependence on slaves that even quite modest households contained two or three slaves, so that to be unable to possess any was, for a man of Philemon's status, a social catastrophe. And it is not unimportant that he was a host for a church, that is, one of those moderately wealthy patrons on whom Paul's churches depended for their finance and accommodation. To maintain a house large enough for a church gathering normally required, in the ancient world, the service of slaves, so that a ban on Christian ownership of (Christian) slaves would have created social and practical difficulties for the church as a whole.

On the other hand, to combine the master–slave relationship with that of brother to brother was hardly a straightforward matter. Of course, everything depends here on what is entailed by being a 'beloved brother', a status that might have purely abstract or ethereal connotations without practical impact on daily life. But if we look elsewhere at what Paul means by 'brotherhood' and how 'brothers' should relate to one another, it appears that the status does have practical implications, for instance in the expectation that brothers 'serve one another in love' (Gal. 5.14) and 'correct one another' (Gal. 6.1). Even if 'brotherhood' in the ancient world did not necessarily entail equality (older brothers had some authority and control over their younger siblings), the expression of mutuality is an important element in Paul's prescription for Christian relationships. And it is this mutuality that would be most difficult to combine with the strictly hierarchical nature of slave-ownership, in which it was very clear (and had to be kept so) what masters could do to slaves and what *could not be done back!* The warning to Christian slaves in 1 Tim. 6.2 not to be disrespectful to their masters because they were 'brothers' indicates how the ethos of mutuality had the potential to disrupt the power relations that undergirded the master–slave relationship.

Thus it is possible that the ambiguities we have noted in the letter to Philemon reflect the difficulties in finding any clear solution to this problem. It is arguable that the tortured 'no longer as a slave but as more than a slave, a beloved brother' indicates Paul's struggle with the problem, in the awareness that the master–slave relationship was impossible to square with that of brother to brother; but the lack of a clear recommendation for manumission may represent his awareness of the difficulties that Philemon, and other church hosts, would face in this regard. Ultimately, of course, we will never know why Paul didn't say something or why he expressed himself so vaguely, but only a realistic notion of what slavery and manumission entailed in the ancient world will enable us to appreciate what was at stake in the various options before Philemon.

One way to appreciate this situation is to imagine how Philemon might have replied to Paul; indeed, it is a useful task to compose such a reply as an imaginative exercise which clarifies how one understands Paul's letter. An interesting example of 'the correspondence continued' was published by Stephen Barton (see Further Reading). Barton imagines that Philemon took Paul's letter to hint at Onesimus's manumission and was shocked at the social implications of this demand. Barton acknowledges that this reading of Paul is influenced by his desire to 'commend as plausible—both historically and, even more so, theologically—the development of Paul towards an ethic of liberation' (p. 98). That only makes explicit the role of theological factors, which may also influence other readings of Philemon. Are others who see Paul here as suggesting manumission, or at least struggling with the anomalous combination of master–slave and brother–brother relationships, influenced by a desire to place Paul within an emancipatory dynamic? Are those who regard Paul's theology as bearing no relation to social status reflecting their own theological judgments? And are those who regard the letter as open-ended laying bare their own unresolved struggles with such issues? Of course, there may be no such correspondence between the interpretation of Paul and the interpreter's own theology, but we would be naive to ignore the hermeneutical processes involved in scholars' suggestions about the outcome of the letter.

What actually happened to Onesimus on his return with this letter we will never know. The fact that the letter has been preserved has suggested to many that it must have had a happy outcome, or at least that Paul's wishes must have been fulfilled. Unfortunately, we don't know who preserved it (Paul, Philemon, Onesimus, others?) nor what the 'happy outcome' might have been. Philemon could have kept the letter as a token of the esteem in which he was held by the apostle, while maintaining Onesimus's slave status in his household. Some slightly romanticized theories have posited that Onesimus preserved the letter as that which won him his freedom. Some explanation has to be given as to how this letter came to be more widely known and incorporated into the Pauline corpus at the time when that was compiled. It is likely that Philemon was preserved largely because of its association with Colossians. If the latter is pseudonymous, we have to posit that someone had access to Philemon quite early and made use of the names listed within it to compose the last chapter of Colossians; it is not likely that Onesimus's private preservation of the letter would have brought that about. If Colossians is authentic, then the two letters belonged together from the beginning and Philemon probably slipped into the canon on the back of its bigger sibling. Knox famously once argued that the letter was preserved by Onesimus, who after his manumission became bishop in Ephesus (a bishop of this name is addressed by Ignatius in his letter to Ephesus at the beginning of the second century). Following Goodspeed, Knox thought that Ephesus was where the Pauline corpus was first compiled, and that Onesimus was personally responsible for the inclusion of this letter about himself. Sadly, we really know nothing about how or where the Pauline corpus came together, and this theory remains purely hypothetical; it also depends on Onesimus living to an extremely advanced age. Moreover, it seems a little disappointing that this emancipated slave oversaw the inclusion of letters that instructed slaves to stay in their place and gave no hint that there was anything anomalous about Christians owning (even Christian) slaves (Col. 3.18–4.1; Eph. 6.5-9; 1 Tim. 6.1-2; Tit. 2.9-10).

Theological Evaluation of the Letter

Since I have already hinted at their significance, it is proper to conclude the analysis of the letter by bringing to the surface some of the factors that have influenced, and continue to influence, theological responses to Philemon.

As just noted, we cannot be sure how Philemon got included in the New Testament canon; its inclusion might have had personal or literary causes quite unrelated to any theological interest in the letter. In fact, its inclusion did not command universal assent even in the fourth century CE, as we can see by the fact John Chrysostom (c. 347–407) and Jerome (c. 342–420) had to defend our text against contemporary criticisms that it was trifling. The way in which they, and Theodore of Mopsuestia, justified its inclusion was to be fateful. Chrysostom found a moral message in the letter, that one should not give up on even the most unpromising people, but he and Theodore also used the letter as an example of Paul's conformity to the legal structures of society: he did not entice Onesimus away from his master, but returned him immediately. In both cases other texts in the Pauline corpus were invoked to back up this interpretation (e.g. Rom. 13.1-7;

1 Cor. 7.21) as the canonizing process smothered whatever subtleties our letter may have contained. Both interpreters felt the need to distance themselves from the 'radical' alternatives advocated by monastic followers of Eustathius and by the Circumcellions, whose challenge to the structures of society led them to encourage slaves to run away. Thus, for apologetic purposes, Paul became the upholder of the social status quo, and the fact that he returned Onesimus with this letter became more important than what he said about the future relationship of master and slave.

For obvious reasons, Philemon has been of only marginal interest in the history of Christian engagement with the New Testament, so that a few such well-respected opinions on the letter easily became normative in the history of interpretation. Luther's treatment of the letter is another case in point. In his preface to the epistle (1522) Luther traced in it a theological paradigm: Paul identified himself with Onesimus to advocate his cause, just as Christ takes our part to reconcile us to God. However, his lectures on Philemon, delivered in 1527, derive a socially conservative lesson from the letter. Onesimus may have run away because he 'wanted to abuse the Christian liberty which he had heard proclaimed, falling into a carnal attitude' (p. 93). In this letter, according to Luther, Paul 'does not release [Onesimus] from his servitude or ask Philemon to do so; indeed he confirms the servitude' (p. 100). Luther's insistence on this point ('You see that slavery is not being abrogated here', p. 101) is not unrelated to the recent Peasants' Revolt and the emergence of the Radical Reformation ('Enthusiasm'), both of which greatly shocked Luther. He thus paraphrases Paul's reassurance to Philemon that Onesimus 'believes and is a beloved brother. Now he will serve with the spontaneous obedience of love, and therefore you will benefit from his having run away' (p. 103). There is nothing here that could possibly justify social upheaval.

The Lutheran tradition, with its tendency to distinguish social from theological spheres ('the two kingdoms'), has continued to influence a long line of German scholarship on Philemon. To take one example, the Lutheran moulding of Lohse's theology is evident in his commentary on Philemon.

As we have seen, Lohse follows those who doubt that either v. 16 or v. 21 has anything to say about the legal aspect of Onesimus's status: 'not a single word is devoted to the question whether the slave should be given his freedom' (p. 206). But that Lohse does not consider this a lack is indicated by his comment on v. 16:

> Although Onesimus 'in the flesh' is, as a slave, the property of his master, this earthly relationship is now surpassed by the union 'in the Lord'. There is no doubt that earthly freedom is a great good. Nevertheless, in the last analysis it is of no significance to the Christian whether he is slave or free. The only thing that matters is to have accepted God's call and to follow him (1 Cor. 7.21-24) (p. 203).

Since both slave and master are under the command of the Lord, their relationship has undergone 'a fundamental change'. Nonetheless, 'although it might seem natural that Philemon grant Onesimus his freedom, the Apostle can leave it to Philemon how he wants to decide. Under all circumstances Philemon is bound to the commandment of love which makes its renovating power effective in any case, since the slave who returns home is now a brother' (p. 203). It seems that, for Lohse, Paul was *right* not to make direct or explicit reference to Onesimus's legal status, since that would be to exaggerate the significance of an 'earthly' phenomenon. In this theological hierarchy of goods, the liberation of a slave is of less significance than the freedom of an owner to follow the commandment of love however 'he wants to decide'.

German scholarship since the 1960s has been rather less content to follow this line; Stuhlmacher's commentary, for instance, agonizes over the legacy of the Lutheran tradition, while still anxious about the dangers of 'enthusiasm'. British and American scholarship has been more deeply influenced by the nineteenth-century struggles over the slave-trade, the abolition of slavery in the British empire and the American civil war. Although the letter to Philemon (and other New Testament passages) were used at the time on *both sides* of the debate over slavery (see Swartley, pp. 31-64), we are all now heirs of the abolitionist movement. Thus in English-speaking scholarship there is a strong presumption that either (1) Paul *did* undermine slavery in this letter to Philemon, at least implicitly, and/or (2) he *would have done so* explicitly if the social circumstances had made that possible. We may briefly examine an example of each of these options. 1. Lightfoot's introduction to his commentary on Philemon is a good example of the first option (pp. 319-29). Declaring that the greatest interest of the letter lies in exhibiting the Christian attitude to slavery, Lightfoot outlines the brutal features of ancient slavery, with which 'Christianity found itself in conflict' (p. 323). Since to prohibit slavery would have 'torn society into shreds', Lightfoot applauds the fact that 'the Apostles never command the liberation of slaves as an absolute duty'. 'Revolutionary violence' is not the spirit of the gospel, which belongs to all time and 'is not concerned with any political or social institutions' (p. 323). Nonetheless, the letter to Philemon, and early Christianity in general, enunciate the principle that all humankind are children of God, 'which must in the end prove fatal to slavery' (p. 325).

> When...the Apostolic precept that 'in Christ is neither bond nor free' was not only recognised but acted upon, then slavery was doomed. Henceforward it was only a question of time. Here was the idea which must act as a solvent, must disintegrate this venerable institution, however deeply rooted and however widely spread (p. 325).

Lightfoot thus pursues traces of evidence for humane attitudes to slaves among early Christians and in Christian imperial legislation, sometimes in overt acts, but 'even more important' in 'the moral and social importance with which the slave was now invested' (p. 326). Thus, although much Christian legislation in this area 'was after all very partial and tentative', and although 'there has been occasional timidity and excess of caution' ('much may be pardoned to men who shrink from seeming to countenance a violent social revolution', p. 328), Christianity was always aiming towards the emancipation of slaves. Hence the abolition of slavery in the British Empire, the liberation of Russian serfs and 'the emancipation of the negro in the vast republic of the New World' are to be hailed as the acme of this progressive history. In Lightfoot's opinion, the letter to Philemon stands as 'the earliest prelude to these magnificent social victories' (p. 329).

Lightfoot's optimistic view of Christian history is open to serious challenge and gains its force from the distorted perspective of hindsight rather than the actual course of events. Slaves transported in their hundreds of thousands across the Atlantic by Christian slave-traders, to be exploited by Christian owners, would have had some reason to doubt this version of events. Indeed, Lightfoot's claim that 'it was only a question of time' betrays a remarkably naive reading of history, which fails to acknowledge the special contribution of the Enlightenment to the Christian change of attitude in the nineteenth century. The notion that Christian imperial legislation shows increasingly humane attitudes to slaves has been challenged in recent scholarship (e.g. Finley), and it has been rightly observed that to treat slaves as 'brothers' without changing their social and legal status could merely *reinforce* the institution of slavery by reducing the impetus to alter social conditions. The Marxist historian, G.E.M. de Ste Croix, is withering in his response to Christian wishful-thinking: 'Whatever the theologian may think of christianity's claim to set free the soul of the slave...the historian cannot deny that it helped to rivet the shackles rather more firmly on his feet' (p. 20). Thus to claim that Philemon was in any straightforward sense a 'prelude' to the emancipation of slaves seems to be insupportable.

2. The other interpretative option noted above was that, although Paul did not appeal for the emancipation of slaves, that was where his heart lay, and he would certainly have done so had social conditions been otherwise. We have already seen an element of this in Lightfoot's statement that 'to prohibit slavery was to tear society into shreds' (p. 323), but, with the loss of confidence in his optimistic reading of history, this element has become more pronounced among apologists for Paul. We may take as representative here the comments by N.T. Wright in the introduction to his commentary. In raising the question 'why...did Paul not protest against the whole dehumanizing system?' (p. 169), Wright excuses Paul on largely pragmatic grounds:

> A loud protest, at that moment in social history, would have functioned simply on the level of the old age... It would, without a doubt, have done more harm than good, making life harder for Christian slaves, and drawing upon the young church exactly the

wrong sort of attention from the authorities. If Paul is jailed for proclaiming 'another king' (Acts 17.7), it must be clear that the kingdom in question is of a different order altogether from that of Caesar. In addition, inveighing against slavery *per se* would have been totally ineffective: one might as well, in modern Western society, protest against the mortgage system. Even if all Christians of Paul's day were suddenly to release their slaves, it is by no means clear that the slaves themselves, or society in general, would benefit: a large body of people suddenly unemployed in the ancient world might not enjoy their freedom as much as they would imagine (p. 169).

This pastiche of explanations is open to challenge on a range of moral and historical counts. The reference to a kingdom 'of a different order' is reminiscent of the Lutheran 'two kingdoms', with its dangerous tendency to leave social and political issues well alone. If slavery were really a moral evil, it is hard to see how one can justify not criticizing it just because it is part of the fabric of society: so was idolatry, and so today is the international debt system which cripples the Third World, but one does not for that reason shrug one's shoulders. More particularly, what is at issue in relation to Paul is not so much why he did not criticize slavery as a whole (though some voices in antiquity certainly did, and Dunn is wrong to claim that 'while *treatment* of slaves was recognized as a moral question, the *fact* of slavery itself was not', p. 306; see Barclay p. 177 and n. 70); what is puzzling is why Paul did not express more clearly the anomaly of *Christian* slave-ownership, particularly the ownership of fellow Christians. To suggest that to emancipate Christian slaves 'suddenly' would cause harmful unemployment is to ignore the careful means by which masters in antiquity could manumit their slaves under terms of continuing employment that benefited both parties.

I have suggested above that there may well have been practical reasons for Paul's hesitancy to recommend that Philemon emancipate the returning Onesimus, though those reasons are more in tune with the realities of first-century society than these put forward by Wright. Even so, one might still register disappointment with Paul's letter from a moral and historical point of view, and it is only Wright's reluctance to do so that can explain this mélange of rationalizations. When he concludes that Paul did undermine slavery, only subtly ('Paul's method is subtler'), his case is no more convincing than that of Lightfoot. According to Wright, Paul knew that it is better to be free than a slave, but

> like Jesus, his way of changing the world is to plant a grain of mustard seed, which, inconspicuous at first, grows into a spreading tree... Like the artist or poet, he does some of his finest work not by the obscure clarity of direct statement, but by veiled allusion and teasing suggestion (pp. 169-70).

One can only weep on behalf of those millions of slaves whose lives might have been immeasurably better had Paul been just a little less 'poetic'. In truth, it seems that apologetics will serve us particularly badly in this area. While we must be careful to understand the multiple facets of slavery and its deep wovenness into the fabric of society and social consciousness in the ancient world, Christian theology may still register its disappointment with Philemon, and the rest of the New Testament, on this score. In suggesting that Paul's phraseology in this letter betrays a more or less conscious struggle over the social implications of the gospel I too may be suffering from a form of wishful thinking, but I would still regret Paul's inability (or unwillingness) to encourage, or even to conceive, different forms of social interdependence, even within the church. Here indeed much hinges on one's understanding of the Christian gospel: is it confined to individual salvation and 'spiritual truths', or has it the power to critique contemporary social practices and the fertility to spawn fresh alternatives? If it proves impotent to challenge obvious institutional evils like slavery, can it hope to correct the many subtler forms of evil that cripple human potential in the various cultures in which Christianity is embedded? For many Christians, the credibility of their faith is at stake in the question whether Philemon, or the New Testament, or the Christian tradition generally, contains the resources which enable the church to critique the distorted ideologies and social injustices of our contemporary society, even if those resources have to be, quite explicitly, developed and applied well beyond their original range. In this respect, both for what it says and for what it does not say, the letter to

Philemon proves to be not only intriguing and beguiling, but also somewhat disturbing.

Further Reading

A valuable survey of the history of interpretation of Philemon can be found at the end of Stuhlmacher's commentary (in German). Luther's preface and lectures may be found (respectively) in *Luther's Works* (Philadelphia: Muhlenberg Press), XXXV (1960), p. 390, and XXIX (1968), pp. 93-105. Other literature cited here is:

Barclay, J.M.G., 'Paul, Philemon and the Dilemma of Christian Slave-Ownership', *NTS* 37 (1991), pp. 161-86.

Barton, S.C., 'Paul and Philemon: A Correspondence Continued', *Theology* 90 (1987), pp. 97-101.

de Ste. Croix, G.E.M., 'Early Christian Attitudes to Property and Slavery', in D. Baker (ed.), *Studies in Church History*, XII (Oxford: Basil Blackwell, 1975), pp. 1-38.

Elliott, N., *Liberating Paul: The Justice of God and the Politics of the Apostle* (BibSem, 27; Sheffield: Sheffield Academic Press, 1995).

Finley, M.I., *Ancient Slavery and Modern Ideology* (London: Chatto & Windus, 1980).

Knox, J., *Philemon among the Letters of Paul* (London: Collins, 1960).

Swartley, W.M., *Slavery, Sabbath, War and Women: Case Studies in Biblical Interpretation* (Scottdale: Herald Press, 1983).

Guides to ancient slavery may be found in:

Bartchy, S.S., *Mallon Chrēsai: First-Century Slavery and the Interpretation of 1 Corinthians 7.21* (Missoula: Scholars Press, 1973).

Bartchy, S.S., 'Slavery, Greco-Roman', *ABD*, VI, pp. 65-73.

Bradley, K.R., *Slaves and Masters in the Roman Empire: A Study in Social Control* (Brussels: Latomus, 1984).

Wiedemann, T., *Greek and Roman Slavery* (London: Croom Helm, 1981).

—*Slavery* (Greece and Rome New Surveys, 19; Oxford: Clarendon Press, 1987).

INDEXES

INDEX OF REFERENCES

OLD TESTAMENT

NEW TESTAMENT

INDEX OF AUTHORS